To PAUL

Eddie

Spiritual Growth
in the Congregation

Spiritual Growth in the Congregation

**by Robert H. Boyte
and Kelly Boyte Peters**

CBP Press
St. Louis, Missouri

© 1988 CBP Press

Library of Congress Cataloging-in-Publication Data

Boyte, Robert H.
    Spiritual growth in the congregation / by Robert H. Boyte and Kelly Boyte Peters.
        108 p.   21.7 cm.
    Bibliography: p. 105
    ISBN 0-8272-3428-7 : $7.95
    1. Spiritual life.   2. Protestant churches.   3. Parishes.
I. Boyte Peters, Kelly.   II. Title.
BV4501.2.B6845 1988
248—dc19   88-9508
                                            CIP

Printed in the United States of America

Contents

To
Mozelle "Dobie" Boyte
mother, grandmother, reader of books
and
Michael Eugene Peters
son, grandson, bearer of hope

Introduction

Worship, nurture, and outreach generate the most activity in Protestant churches. Regardless of size or location, these churches make major efforts to provide experiences of worship, opportunities for growth, and avenues of service for their members and friends.

Even the most simple service of worship requires support activities that may surprise the casual worshiper. Hymnals, musical instruments, worship leaflets, elements for Holy Communion, rehearsals for musicians, and schedules for ushers and others who will serve are only a few of the necessary provisions for a typical worship service.

A program of education calls for people to provide space, plan educational experiences, and secure materials ranging from modeling clay to video equipment. Before the first student arrives, leaders will have met several times to form lesson plans and a schedule of events. A typical program of nurture will provide cribs in the nursery for the youngest and barrier-free entrances for those with special needs.

But the typical Protestant church extends itself to serve others in a mission of concern and love. Some parishes provide their neighborhoods with housing, daily meals, food pantries, day care, and recreational and enrichment opportunities for the elderly and the disabled. Congregations that are not activity centers sponsor many events to support benevolence and mission budgets to provide money for denominational and ecumenical outreach projects on this continent and around the world.

Worship and nurture and outreach are the basic components of the Protestant church. They require a great deal of activity. Yet a quick study of the typical Protestant church would produce an impressive list of other opportunities and activities. The list would include sewing, bowling, softball, basketball, travel, discussion of the great books, music appreciation, painting, crafts, handbells, exercise, Alcoholics Anonymous and Al-Anon, Boy Scouts, swimming, choruses, grief counseling, individual and group therapy, book reviews, nutrition classes, financial planning, citizenship classes, drama groups, parenting classes, and retirement planning.

Churches provide these additional activities in order to serve their members. Often the members themselves encourage the activities by saying, "We ought to offer a class in photography. There are a lot of shutterbugs around here." The alert congregation senses where its members are and provides help at each step along the road of life. Classes on parenting, financial planning, and preparation for retirement are typical ways the congregation says to its members, "We care about you!" By offering a wide variety of programs, a congregation presents an attractive profile for prospective members. New people like to associate with a church that shows it has energy and imagination to provide programs for people of every age and condition.

Congregations also provide a variety of programs to serve the community. They accept responsibility for their community and do what they can to serve, inform, and enrich their neighbors even when these activities do not directly help the church.

Like the traditional programs of worship, education, and outreach, these "auxiliary" activities also represent investments of time and money. To make the programs happen, people must join together to plan the activities, provide the leadership, and arrange for the financing. Space must be provided. Equipment and supplies must be secured. Matters of insurance and liability demand attention. The programs must be announced, promoted, and advertised. Supervision and evaluation must take place.

By providing traditional services and auxiliary programs, the typical Protestant church has become a center of activity. This book does not intend to criticize the church as a center of activity. It applauds those alert congregations that creatively seek new ways to be lively and responsive. But this book asks, "Is activity enough?" "Can the church's mission be fulfilled with a busy calendar alone?" For many people, their church is a center of activity, but it is not a center of meaning. Thus church life participates in the disintegration of personal and family life and heightens the accumulation of stress in its members while they find life's meaning symbolized by hearth, flag, and corporation — but not by the altar.

While mainstream Protestant groups have widened their range of programs, other groups have dealt with the matter of meaning. Fundamentalist groups have preached their formulas for meaning in storefront chapels, shiny suburban cathedrals, and glitzy talk-show settings. Charismatic groups have promised experiences whose intensity invalidates any reflective quest for meaning. Various forms of Catholicism and Eastern religious groups have provided solitude, meditation techniques, guided retreats, and fasting as ways to enter the realm of meaning and truth.

Protestant church planners may have misread the signs that members were flashing. People may have asked for familiar programs when what they really wanted were answers to deep questions. Topical programs that have clogged church calendars may have been the search for meaning in disguise. Too embarrassed to confess their hunger for spiritual reflection, the people asked for classes in parenting or retirement planning. The request for Bible study is a case in point. When lay people ask for Bible study, they are wanting direct engagement with the Word of God. What is offered in return is often a course in the documentary theory of the Pentateuch or the missionary journeys of Paul.

But the desire for a deeper understanding of life's meaning can be clearly seen now. The issue has broken out of the clouds of embarrassment and is now clearly visible: Spirituality is needed in mainstream Protestantism.

The development of spirituality in a congregation is a risky effort; that gamble should be recognized from the beginning. In any congregation a group seeking "life together" may find itself leading a "life apart" from the rest of the church. Members of such groups are often surprised to discover that the congregation's suspicion has led to mistrust and finally to alienation. Even the word *spiritual* suggests that there are those who are *unspiritual* and thus of lesser value.

Because the need for spirituality has been recognized, a growing stream of resources is flowing from denominational and private sources. A congregation intending to probe the spiritual life will have a wide assortment of books, study guides, films, videocassettes, audiocassettes, speakers, and retreat formats from which to choose.

11

And the choosing is the problem! The aim of this book is to help a congregation create the climate where spirituality may thrive and the people of God may grow in faith, unity, love, and peace.

1

The Ordered Life in a Disorderly Time

When the phone rang just after dinner, Bryan expected to hear someone trying to sell aluminum siding or resort property. Instead it was Marge Jackson of the church nominating committee.

Returning to the family room, he told Susan, "They want me to head the church 'Worship and Spiritual Life Committee' next year. I told them I'd think about it and get back to them in a couple of days."

"How do you feel about it now?" Susan asked.

Bryan replied, "The worship part doesn't bother me. I'd just have to work with the choir director, see that the organ is tuned, and see that people are reasonably happy with the hymns we sing. But it's the 'spiritual life' part that troubles me."

Before he went to sleep that night, memories of his own religious experiences came to Bryan. He remembered counting all the organ pipes Sunday after Sunday in the old church where he grew up. He also remembered Consecration Night at high school conference. He thought of his college roommate who joined the Campus Crusade for Christ and of the guy across the hall who joined the Hare Krishna movement. The last time he saw him he was asking for money at the airport.

Bryan thought of Marge's call again as he drove to the shop. He wished there were a better description of the "spiritual life" part of that job. Did they want him to organize a vigil for peace, start Wednesday-night prayer meetings, develop a chain of prayer for the sick — or something else?

He thought it strange that something that seemed such a natural part of church life should be so hard to describe.

Guideline: *A congregation seeking to develop the spirituality of its members will be realistic about life today and the struggles and longings of its members.*

One of the earliest writers in the field of spirituality was Gregory of Nyssa in the fourth century. In Gregory's time, a pilgrimage to Jerusalem was regarded as a spiritual experience that every lover of Christ should seek. But Gregory challenged the prevailing view. He observed that since the pilgrimage was not something ordered by Jesus, it did not deserve the importance it had acquired.

But Gregory had other reasons for discounting the trek to Jerusalem. In his time such travel was exceedingly difficult and dangerous. Given those dangers and the customs of the time, it was unrealistic to expect women to undertake such a venture. Gregory declared that "the holy life is open to all, men and women alike" and opposed any spiritual exercise that was not available to both men and women.

Gregory was uncommonly sensible about the spiritual life as well as centuries ahead of his time in recognizing the rights of women. He did not advocate spiritual practices that simply called attention to those who completed them. He once said, "Of the contemplative life, the peculiar mark is modesty."

A program for spirituality today should reflect the sensitivity and sensibility that Gregory stood for in his time. When a congregation embarks upon a course leading to deepened spiritual awareness, it will stay in touch with each of its members, ensuring that growth is available to all of them. A contemporary program of spirituality will reflect the complexities of the contemporary world, and such a program should relate closely to the lifestyles and issues in the lives of church members. In order that we may develop an appropriate climate for spiritual growth that relates to personal experience, let us examine the world in which we live and the particular issues that greet church members daily.

Signs of the Times
Cult of Youth

Since the early 1980s, sociologists have made us aware that

America is growing older. Every contemporary news magazine documents "the graying of America." People are living longer, and there are more elderly among our population than ever before. Yet the very pages of those magazines display, through advertising, the belief that youth is to be worshiped. There is a contradictory message here that perplexes us and affects our behavior.

Some young people, susceptible to the worship of youth, are afraid to grow older, and thus act immaturely, unwilling or unable to assume the responsibilities of adulthood. Others see the depictions of the glamorous lifestyles of young men and women and wonder why their lives do not measure up.

Perhaps it is the fear of death that grips us as a society and renders us incapable of assessing the needs or appreciating the abilities of older people. The facts are that millions of older Americans long to give of their wisdom and experience, while millions more struggle with the basic necessities of daily life.

As a result, we segregate ourselves from each other, and younger people alienate themselves from their own futures. A spiritual program, set in a congregation, can help make sense of this particular confusion. Through study and introspection we become aware of the gifts and idolatries of each particular stage in life. Ideally, the congregation is the family that sees beyond age categories, helping people to break out of their own groups and prejudices. We appreciate the support we give each other for our individual struggles, and we go into the world prepared to face the "cult of youth" with our own mature knowledge of the value of each individual, regardless of age.

Time

The amount of time people have and how they spend that time must be kept in mind by those concerned about the spiritual life. Both quality and quantity must be studied.

Tilden Edwards describes the quality of time today:

> The day is a kaleidoscope of bits and pieces connected by nothing, expressing no real common ground. The result is a kind of personal and societal fragmentation, a desperate and futile effort to hold it all together, a pathless, complex jungle that leaves so many people insecure, angry, frightened, confused, and easy prey for the first simplistic savior that comes along.[1]

15

We know that a full calendar of activities is no guarantee that any of them will contain meaning or real satisfaction, and is often an attempt to mask the sense of futility. We complain about being too busy, but if we are honest, we know we are more comfortable that way. People whose lives have been full of work, taking care of children, and related activities look forward to an early retirement, only to find that, with hours to fill, they have lost their identity and purpose.

In another era, meaning was given to hours and days through the *Rule of St. Benedict*, which provided a pattern for ordering the Christian life. The Rule linked the rhythm of nature to the worship of Christ, and the needs of the community to the needs of the individual.

> For the monk of St. Benedict, the needs of the monastery and his own talents determined the nature of the tasks he would perform. He was subject to the rhythms of the earth and the patterns of darkness and light in his work as he was subject to the rhythms of the Church in his formal prayer. Together the patterns formed a whole and healing life rhythm. The dynamic balance of forces allowed each man to become his best self if he chose to submit to them.[2]

We envy the simplicity of such a lifestyle and it *is* possible for us to develop a more calm and ordered life as we develop spiritually. As we grow more comfortable with ourselves, we learn the possibility of being alone without being lonely. In discovering the value of personal relationships, we desire to be with each other without always including the trappings of activity and noise. The spirituality centered in the congregation will help us order life's moments and activities according to our new-found values.

Family

Not too many years ago, a discussion of the spiritual life might have included a section on relating to the "givens" of family life: the working father, the homemaker mother, sibling rivalries, etc. Today, a spiritual life will relate to the realities of family life in a time when there are no givens. The family tree has been redesigned to include places for step-parents and children born to single parents. Living in a family has always been difficult, but without the assurance of lifelong commitments it is particularly fraught with tension today.

As the family structures have splintered, people have felt freer to question all of life's loyalties, including faith commitments. When one of the basic relationships is broken, some respond by finding no sense in the world. They long to find a place or a way "to fit all of the pieces together again." Some men and women look to the church to provide the security and the identity once found at home.

Survival

People in the closing years of the twentieth century are conditioned by survival. Our memories are scorched by the fires of those who did not survive Auschwitz, and our ears are burned by the stories of those who did. Film clips replay the destruction of Hiroshima, and television cameras show the bodies of those who are starving in Africa. Stories of personal violence and child abuse remind us that none of us is immune from the brutality of our time. The question of survival comes up daily as defense budgets, nuclear arms, environmental pollution, and urban violence are routinely reported. Children who once daydreamed about "what I'll be when I grow up" wonder matter-of-factly if they will grow up. Adults question the wisdom of having children in such a time, wondering not only about their survival but also about the quality of life they will face.

Despite great temptation, our spirituality must not let us escape the tragedies of this world by dreaming about another one. Neither can we dull our senses with a cheery brand of positive thinking that does not take our experiences seriously. Rather, our spirituality will call us into deeper and more rewarding relationships with God and with one another. Like Job, we will be given the assurance, not that our problems will disappear, but that God will be with us through each of them. Growing in relationship with one another reminds us of the joy our world still has to give and offers a healthy balance to our feelings of despair. Finally, our spirituality calls us into the world, not with unrealistic hopes, but with purposeful action rooted in prayer.

Loneliness

The urgency of the survival question is shaped by the loneliness of those who ask it. People are not asking, "Will we survive?" They are asking, "Will I survive?" Many observers have found loneliness to be a peculiar mark of twentieth-century life in North America. Edward Hopper preserved urban loneliness in his paintings of all-night diners in the big city. Tennessee Williams found loneliness in the South. Folk songs report loneliness among the poor in Appalachia. The loneliness of young people is given a voice and a shriek in rock music. Garrison Keillor tells us that loneliness exists among "Norwegian bachelor farmers" and the "shy people of Lake Wobegon."

In a careful sociological study, Suzanne Gordon distinguishes between aloneness and loneliness. Aloneness is to be expected as a condition of being human. Loneliness, however, is a pathological condition. It is a comprehensive experience that controls a person's self-understanding and his or her relationships with others. [3]

Churches certainly have their share of lonely people who, while sitting in a pew surrounded by others, feel totally alone. The person on the spiritual walk can see fellow worshipers as traveling companions, each encountering joys and sorrows, each needing support and encouragement. Spirituality encourages solitude as well as a time to draw upon one's inner resources and face one's vulnerability. It is to be hoped that those who grow spiritually will grow in sensitivity towards others. Thus, after we have embarked on our walk, we will learn to look for those in our midst who seem estranged and welcome them in a genuine and nonthreatening manner.

What Is Spirituality?

It is only after we understand our world that we can begin to describe what we mean by spirituality. We are seeking that which will give meaning to our everyday experiences, our persisting fears, and our lingering questions.

Spirituality is an attitude toward life, a perspective on life, a way of being in the world. As we grow spiritually, we learn to give meaning to our common experiences. Spirituality is a lens through which we see God acting in our world. Rooted in our common life experiences, it preserves the mystery of life and our relationship with God but demystifies it.

The appropriate goal of a spiritual life is not to experience more emotional highs or moments of ecstasy, but to be more aware of the sacredness of all of life's moments and relationships.

> We should not seek experiences, but should pay attention to those we have. We should not cultivate ecstasies, but should remain open to the lessons they offer us. In short, we should live our lives in an awake, aware fashion, honestly claiming for ourselves what belongs to us: our joy, our pain, our generous impulses, our anger. By authentically claiming our experiences, we can begin to come into relationship with them, and through this process, further our path to spirituality.[4]

Spirituality is an inward walk, whereby we reacquaint ourselves with our sacred history, peel away the layers of resistance, and prepare ourselves for God's presence. We are not solitary creatures, however, and our walk is not only an inward one. We relate to God as we relate to the world around us, simultaneously enlarging our understanding of God, and acting in love and responsibility towards God's world.

As thus described, it seems that spirituality is a quality that should be present in every facet of the church's life. So why the new interest in spirituality? Why is it that so many religious books published recently include the word *spirituality* in their titles? Why are we discussing spirituality as if it were a lost treasure, recently rediscovered? Is it not something that has always been a part of the life of the church?

According to Martin Marty, the history of the American Protestant churches cannot be understood except as it specifically correlates with events in American history. That is, American Protestant thought and action has always developed in close relation to political and social events. Protestants have been interested not only in establishing churches and sustaining a meaningful faith system but also in ensuring that their faith system worked to the good of the country. And correspondingly, they wanted the laws, attitudes, and actions of the nation to reflect, at least in a general way, their value system. For example, in the first half of the nineteenth century, most Americans were conventional Protestants who had turned "the nation into a kind of a church." Marty further describes them: "Pleased with their nation, they wanted it to be somehow homogeneous — a land of shared values and world views encouraging public virtue in the context of a believable world system."[5]

This meshing of faith and "public virtue" is often referred to as public religion or civil religion. Most date the beginning of American civil religion to the Revolutionary period. Benjamin Franklin was a strong advocate of a faith that would be useful to the public. "It would be advantageous in promoting a religious character among private persons."[6] From its inception, American civil religion was not a carefully designed system of definitions and commandments, but rather a conglomeration of least common denominators, beliefs that most religions agreed upon and that would be beneficial attributes for citizens to acquire. In civil religion, "reason . . . counted more than faith, and morals more than grace."[7]

Every church in the United States has both assimilated some civil religion into its faith and practice and has stood against it. One way of understanding American Protestantism is to chronicle how churches have stood in relation to the public religion. One conclusion is clear. Events in American political life have a direct and distinct impact upon American religious life. This is a relationship unique to the United States.

In other countries, religion reacts to the state as a separate entity. For example, in a Latin American country at war, some church people will call for the immediate defense of their country, whereas others will call for a pacific resistance to the state. Either action is seen as the church's response to the state. In the United States, however, the announcement of war has an automatic effect on the very belief systems of Christians. For all of us have, to some degree, incorporated American civil religion into our ways of believing. We can attempt to stand outside and praise or criticize the state, but we can never be objective.

When we North Americans test our religious sensibility, we must not only ask the questions "How do we feel about God?" and "How is God at work in the world?" but also "How do we feel about our nation and its current actions?" Failure to ask this last question will leave an important element in our faith system unexamined.

In *The Broken Covenant* (1975), Robert Bellah describes

American civil religion in terms of a covenant.[8] Loosely stated, his description is that the early proponents of civil religion thought of Americans as the new chosen people, whom God had promised a good life in the new land. For their part, the American people had to live by certain basic moral principles. Thus, as long as things were perceived to be "going well," Americans thought they were living up to their part of the covenant. There were swings and shifts, but for nearly two centuries American Protestantism was on a fairly even keel.

According to Bellah, things changed sometime in the 1960s. Many events led to the questioning of the basic perception of well-being. Attention was paid to the poor, who would never know the fulfillment of the promise of economic security. Groups long ignored made bold statements, reminding Americans that the promise of "liberty and justice for all" was far from being a reality. Environmental experts began telling us that some of our land and water had been damaged, perhaps irreparably. Third World countries complained about the multinational corporations who took advantage of their people. Finally, America was deeply involved in a controversial and costly war. From all sides, the covenant began to crumble.

In the 1970s, every firmly held principle was challenged. Drugs were a problem for every group, at every age-level. Premarital sex was common. Teen pregnancy was epidemic. The experience of Watergate led to a suspicion of public officials and other authority figures.

The events of the 1960s and 1970s left our nation wondering, *What have we done to deserve this?* If there was a covenant, then it was surely broken. The fabric of society had been shredded. The principles and the basic moral values around which civil religion had formed were each called into question.

During these two decades, a new kind of religious awakening occurred. Perhaps people were searching for a replacement for the broken covenant. Perhaps they were trying to put the fabric of civil religion back together again. On every front there appeared a search for spiritual roots and strength. Fundamentalist churches began to show growth in numbers. Young people turned to Eastern religions, to Jesus movements, and to cults. A charismatic renewal began in the Catholic church. Mainline Protestant churches, having heard the cries of those long forgotten, sought to bring fairness to the nation's laws and to their own church structures. Equal opportunity for minorities, ordination for women, and better living standards for the poor were advocated.

In the 1980s, we find the social and political mood of our nation somewhat calmer, at least on the surface. Yet it is not clear that the covenant has been restored or that the civil religion is being articulated clearly. Rather, the American Protestant churches seem to be more divided than ever before. Two distinct camps have emerged, reflecting the disparate sides of the covenant. Conservatives have become more active in the political arena, demanding that their voices be heard at long last. Mainline churches are re-establishing groups and networks that in the previous two decades called for the nation to work for peace and justice.

This history is the context that forms the answer to the question, "Why the renewed interest in spirituality?" As was discussed at the beginning of the chapter, we live in difficult times. Responsible people of faith feel compelled to live their daily lives in a conscious, careful way. They want to understand contemporary political events and formulate their responses to those events based on a strong faith. It is not enough to live as "good citizens" or "good Christians." Rather, it is time to examine what we mean by those terms and redefine them. So Christians are coming to their churches to look for a way to articulate their faith and ethics in a manner appropriate to the times in which we live.

We are concentrating our discussion primarily on the mainline Protestant churches, since that is the group of churches with which we are most familiar. There are particular reasons for the members and clergy of such churches to be engaged in the search for spirituality. Spirituality has been practically left out of the agenda of most of the mainline Protestant churches during the past several decades. Christian education has focused more on understanding the world and less on understanding our faith. Preaching has not helped to articulate our faith systems but has been built upon presuppositions never fully explained nor understood. Certain questions basic to the development of spiritually mature people have not been asked in our churches. Thus, our young people and adults, and some clergy, cannot begin to explain what God means to them, why or how they pray, and how they understand sin, forgiveness, or grace.

Mainline Protestants may shudder at the tactics of the funda-

mentalists, or laugh at the worship practices of the more conserva-
tive Christians, but these groups are undeniably better at articulating their faith. Similarly, Roman Catholics, brought to life by the
events of Vatican II, can eloquently articulate the relationship of
their faith to issues such as ecumenism, social justice, and the
ordination of women. Whether they be charismatics or devotees of
Thomas Merton, the Roman Catholic community in America
today is able to express itself in areas where the Protestants cannot
seem to find words.

The members and the clergy in the mainline Protestant
churches have recognized that spirituality is an area in which they
have fallen behind. The search for an authentic spiritual life is now
underway. It will not deter the efforts in social justice or evangelism but will give those efforts new meaning. In order to share
effectively with others the love of God in our complicated world,
we need a strong relationship with God and an ability to articulate
our faith. The interest in spirituality is also based upon a healthy
sense of power and responsibility on the part of the laity, who are
no longer satisfied to have spiritual health "trickle down" from the
pulpit but who want to take an active role in their spiritual lives. A
renewal of spirituality will not lessen the importance of our
relationship to civil religion. Rather, it is to be hoped that our
spiritual strength will encourage us to pursue liberty and justice
with renewed vigor.

As reading any of the spiritual masters shows, spiritual growth
is often treacherous. We feel vulnerable, we question our experiences, and we find coping with the triviality and brutality of this
world increasingly difficult. It is for these reasons and others that
we suggest that no one begin the walk alone. The congregation, the
community of faith, is the ideal setting in which to grow spiritually.

Our spiritual journey will strengthen us as individuals and will
give a new sense of meaning and purpose to our lives. If we take
our spiritual walk alone, not only do we find the walk dangerous,
but we risk losing our sense of purpose. The appropriate purpose is
not just to feel good personally, but to find all of our relationships
enhanced. Since we live in a world of interconnectedness, our
spiritual walk is not one to be taken alone. In the congregation, we
discover our purpose along with others, each providing personal
insight along the way. When our experience of spiritual growth is
centered in the congregation, we are making a commitment to the

church. We find the resources of the church at our disposal and can discover our spiritual lives enriched not only through worship and prayer but also through education, outreach, and fellowship.

The Cry . . . Disguised and Persistent

The need for a deeper spiritual encounter is not always expressed in clear language. Often behavior that disrupts normal congregational life is really a cry for religion that is more personal and less organizational. Sometimes people withdraw from church activities not because they are angry or hurt, but because they long for engagement at a level deeper than the church is providing.

Church leaders must be sensitive to those cries of spiritual hunger even when they are disquieting and disruptive. They need to be appreciated for their intensity and persistence.

Much of European culture can be traced to the Benedictine monasteries, which were centers of industry and letters as well as prayer. The *Rule of St. Benedict* appeared at a time when the hunger for a fuller life caused people to stand in line begging for admission into the monastery. Here is how the monastery was to respond to the request for entry:

> When anyone is newly come for the reformation of his life, let him not be granted an easy entrance. [Instead, if the newcomer] perseveres in his knocking and if it is seen, after four or five days that he bears patiently the harsh treatment and the difficulty of admission, and that he persists in his petition, then let entrance be granted him.[9]

There are people in Protestant churches today who share the same desire for a spiritual life as those persistent people at the monastery's gate, even though they express their longing in less dramatic ways.

Beginning a program of spiritual enrichment is not like beginning any other program in the church. In fact, it is so different, we hesitate to call it a program. It should be recognized from the outset that there will be no definite timeline for spiritual growth. Individuals will walk at their own pace and no "progress" will be measured. Likewise there will never be a time when the program is completed.

Still, we should be aware of the expectations we have for our spiritual lives, for though we will not measure progress, people will want to see some form of results. Our program, too, will have more structure and meaning if we keep some sort of goals in mind. It is suggested that the desired results be discussed from the beginning and that exercises designed to relate to those results be incorporated into the program. For example, if one individual states a desire to understand more about the Holy Spirit, plans could include reading various definitions of the Holy Spirit and encouraging that individual to express his or her own opinions on what has been read.

The desire for easy answers, for "a better life," for help with life crises, are legitimate wants and should not be condemned. A church member turns on the television set and hears a preacher promise all the answers, all the solutions. Then she or he comes to church wondering how we can compete. We should welcome the individual who turns off the television set and turns instead to us. We will offer an authentic, noncompetitive approach, sensitive to the needs of each individual. We will not claim to produce results but will attempt to be faithful as we see God at work and are open to the presence of God's spirit in our lives.

A certain intensity often accompanies spiritual growth, and the strongly felt experiences of a "spiritually alive" group can often lead to serious conflicts within a congregation. To avoid such a problem, we can hold up spiritual growth as an area of concern for the entire congregation and not the sole property of one group within the church. Specifically, we would suggest that a congregation embark upon this walk together, and include the participation of every group within the church.

A program for spirituality will understand the conditions under which today's Christians live. It will keep in mind their family structures, their time commitments, their worries and fears, and what they hope to gain. It will relate our systems of believing to the realities of the contemporary world. Spirituality today will not be tempted to reconstitute the time of Benedict or of Norman Rockwell. It will reflect the realities of today's world and today's believers.

2

"You Have Searched Me and Known Me"

Sharon had looked forward to the district women's prayer retreat for months. It was to be a time when she could develop her own life of prayer and explore the depths of her inner self — depths she knew were there but she was too busy to take seriously. She longed to share her experiences in prayer with other women and allow the resources of the Bible to nourish her spirit. As she packed her clothes, her Bible, and her notebook, Brad and the children came in to tell her good-bye and wish her a good weekend.

As she nosed the car up the narrow driveway on Sunday night, she wondered what she should tell her family. Yes, she had enjoyed herself. Yes, she did meet many other women who shared her interests. Yes, the food was good and the camp setting peaceful.

But she had expected so much more! She had hoped to reach a spiritual mountaintop. She had hoped to experience the presence of God intensely, intimately. Not only had she longed for God to address her, Sharon, personally; she had expected to become so close to God, she would even forget who she was and forget all the concerns she carried with her each day.

Not even Brad would understand the disappointment Sharon felt, for he had not known the hopes she had taken with her. Sharon decided to report on only the good parts of the retreat. She hoped Brad would not notice the disappointment she felt so keenly.

Guideline: *A congregation seeking to develop the spirituality of its members will help them maintain the distinctiveness of their individual lives and recognize the unity of body and spirit.*

Spirituality deals with relationships. It involves our relationship with God, and it includes our understanding of ourselves as we encounter God. Now is the time to ask: What can we expect from a growing spirituality? Must we decrease so that the Divine might increase? Will our own selves shrink as we become more and more absorbed with God?

Readers of the Psalms recognize that relationship with God gives a person a new self-understanding. Spiritual discovery takes place as the individual encounters God.

> Whither shall I go from thy Spirit?
>> Or whither shall I flee from thy presence? . . .
> If I take the wings of the morning
>> and dwell in the uttermost parts of the sea,
> even there thy hand shall lead me,
>> and thy right hand shall hold me. . . .
> For thou didst form my inward parts,
>> thou didst knit me together in my mother's womb.
> I praise thee, for thou art fearful and wonderful.
>> Wonderful are thy works!
> Thou knowest me right well;
>> my frame was not hidden from thee,
> when I was being made in secret,
>> intricately wrought in the depths of the earth. (Psalms 139:7, 9-10, 13-15)

The encounter with God gives the worshiper the insight and courage required for honest self-evaluation. In Psalm 51 the writer is able to confess sin and anticipate the joy of forgiveness because of the new awareness that prayer provides:

> Behold, thou desirest truth in the inward being;
>> therefore teach me wisdom in my secret heart.
> Purge me with hyssop, and I shall be clean;
>> wash me, and I shall be whiter than snow.
> Fill me with joy and gladness;
>> let the bones which thou hast broken rejoice.
> Hide thy face from my sins,
>> and blot out all my iniquities.
>
> Create in me a clean heart, 0 God,
>> and put a new and right spirit within me.

Cast me not away from thy presence,
>and take not thy holy Spirit from me.
Restore to me the joy of thy salvation,
>and uphold me with a willing spirit. (Psalm 51:6-12)

In this book we seek a spirituality that affirms the value of the individual in her or his relationship with the Divine. This vision of spirituality sees that human life is not a dualism in which the body struggles with the soul, or matter with spirit. It understands human personality as a dynamic unity of body and spirit.

Advocates of the Personal

Ground was broken for Protestant spirituality two hundred years before Martin Luther (1483-1546) strode on the scene. Meister Eckhart (ca. 1260-1327) was the father of the movement that came to be known as the "Rhineland mystics." Eckhart and his followers identified many of the issues that would later become the rallying cry of Luther and others. Two of these were the need for the institutional reform of the church and a cleansing of the corrupt clergy.

But students of the period note "an even deeper community of values and ideas" linking the Rhineland mystics with Luther and his followers. This was the agreement that the knowledge of ultimate reality is "intensely and unavoidably personal." [10]

Union with God was Eckhart's strongest point. "Eckhart's great aim as preacher and religious teacher was to promote the Christian's union with God. This he counted as the end of all religion and the essence of salvation as brought to the world by Jesus Christ. In his own person, Christ united God and humanity and thus made it possible for humanity to become one with God. Eckhart interpreted union with God in the most intimate possible sense. It is not simply communion with God, or oneness of will and affection with him, but a complete fusion of man's nature with the nature of God." [11]

Luther's link with Meister Eckhart was established through John Tauler who was a follower of Eckhart. In fact, Luther was reading the sermons of Tauler just before the publication of his famous ninety-five theses.

But Luther did not go all the way with Eckhart. Although he

pleaded for an encounter with God, Luther did not want to see the individual dissolve into the Divine. Justification by faith, the essential doctrine of the Reformation, assumes that the individual has an authentic place before the God of judgment and grace. For Luther it was "justification" not "fusion" that was to be prized.

John Calvin (1509-1564), leader of the Genevan wing of the Reformation, placed even greater distance between the Reformation and the German mystics, due in part to Calvin's own background in humanism. Although Calvin believed in the indwelling of Christ, he was careful to "exclude any mystic connotation that might diminish the distance between God and man. Calvin wished to avoid the anthromorphism of the Rhineland mystics, who found a bit of God in every man, which leads to a mystical union with the creator."[12]

We are tempted to develop religious feelings that would blur the distinction between the human and the Divine. Every person longs for union with God, especially in difficult times. When we compare our personal inadequacy with God's power, we long to unite with the Divine. When we confront a dying planet and consider our poor care of the earth and its creatures, we long to unite with the Divine. When we realize the brevity of life and contemplate our own death, we long to unite with the Divine. When we anticipate the violent destruction of all life on earth through nuclear attack or accident, union with God seems most attractive.

In recent years there has been an increasing interest in Eastern religious practices by many in the West. Established religions, such as Hinduism and Buddhism, and new religious movements with Eastern roots, such as Hare Krishna, have attracted many, especially young people. These religious groups offer their followers the possibility of the union of their souls with the Divine and the loss of their personal identity in the worship practices of the group.

Thomas Merton (1915-1968), our century's most famous mystic, often wrote of union with God, a promise that seemed more alluring toward the end of his life as Merton learned more and more about Buddhism. It is worth noting that Thomas Merton was summoned less frequently by his social conscience as he grew in his fascination by and identification with the religions of the East.

29

Merton's book *Contemplative Prayer* was written with monks in mind, though he welcomed other readers too. This is one of his most serious works, published after his death. In this book he writes of the disappearance of the individual:

> The unitive knowledge of God is not a knowledge of an object by a subject, but a far different and transcendent kind of knowledge in which the created "self" which we all are seems to disappear in God and to know him alone. In passive purification then the self undergoes a kind of emptying and an apparent destruction, until, reduced to emptiness it no longer knows itself, apart from God.[13]

To advocate the personal is not to ignore the excesses of individualism. These excesses have been identified by many observers and published in many books, most recently in *Habits of the Heart*. Although religious individualism is rooted in seventeenth-century America, it had rapid growth in "the peculiarly American phenomenon of revivalism," with its insistence on personal experience to the exclusion of any other mode of Christian discipline.

Prominent public figures have given added weight to individualism in American religious life:

> Thomas Jefferson said, "I am a sect myself," and Thomas Paine, "My mind is my church." Many of the most influential figures in nineteenth-century American culture could find a home in none of the existing religious bodies, though they were attracted to the religious teaching of several traditions. One thinks of Ralph Waldo Emerson, Henry David Thoreau, and Walt Whitman.[14]

The same study uncovered an extreme case of religious individualism in our day, that of a person identified as Sheila Larson. Her confession illustrates how individualism can easily slide into privatism. "I believe in God. I'm not a religious fanatic. I can't remember the last time I went to church. My faith has carried me a long way. It's Sheilaism. Just my own little voice."[15]

Excessive individualism deprives the person of a vision of the world made sacred by God's creative act and the sacrificial love of Christ on the cross. Spirituality today must not yield to undifferentiated mysticism merely to avoid the excesses of privatism. "We are living in the era of the person. The value of the human person in all his uniqueness and freedom is perhaps the single most influential discovery of modern man."[16]

Living in the world created by God and redeemed by Christ enables every believer to have a vocation that transcends personal goals and individual needs. As Teilhard de Chardin wrote to a friend, "What we have to learn is to preserve a real appetite for life and action while at the same time renouncing once and for all any desire to be happy just for ourselves."[17]

A Unity of Body and Spirit

Spirituality as practiced through the centuries has often become a mysticism made successful by the blending of the self into the Divine. But this form of spirituality fails to consider the meaning and purpose of creation and incarnation and robs life of its meaning and usefulness in the world of God's creation and redemption.

But what is this "self" that retains individuality while living in God's love after the manner of Jesus the Christ? Is it a soul encased in a body, which returns to the Creator at the death of the body? Or is the life of the Spirit a way to protect the eternal, immaterial soul from the influence of matter in order that the soul may remain unstained for its entry into heaven?

A recent study of Christian history calls such a view of spirituality "the old asceticism." This old asceticism, a position developed by St. Augustine (354-430), featured "a closed energy system." As Augustine put it, "When the soul grows strong, the body withers; when the body grows strong the soul withers."

This dualism is in contrast to the language of the Scriptures, which sees the conflict not between the body and the soul but between the flesh and the spirit, with the body as the prize. The "flesh" as here understood is not the body, nor the covering of the body. "Flesh" is whatever in life is invested with more meaning than it can actually provide. Margaret R. Miles notes that the apostle Paul gave "the desperate and unconscious demand" the title, "the flesh."

The difficulty has arisen when Christian writers have substituted *body* and *soul* for *flesh* and *spirit*. "Soul is then severely differentiated from body as the location of spirit, and body is carelessly identified with the flesh that possesses it."[18] Writes Miles:

This language confuses and frustrates us by contradicting the metaphysical affirmation of the human body to which the Christian authors are committed by Christian doctrine. The "old asceticism" is the result of the collapse of the Pauline language of spirit and flesh into that of soul and body.[19]

The need, Miles says, is for a "new asceticism" that will understand the body in biblical terms. The new asceticism based on the intimate relationship of body and soul means that when the body is charged by ascetic practices the soul too would be affected.[20]

The new asceticism provides opportunities for fresh programming for the local church. Seeking to minister to the whole person, a congregation may offer exercise and dance classes, painting, and pottery classes, and nutrition and diet counseling. These classes would be offered not as a way to present an attractive image in the community but as an integral part of a total ministry.

Churches can also examine the way they get things done to determine if their procedures contribute to the wholeness of the members. Whether we examine the structures of denominations or the organizational charts of local churches, we gather evidence to show how church structures perpetuate a view of the world that is divided and not holistic.

In order to achieve necessary objectives, church people divide into groups to promote activities in worship, outreach, education, social concerns, and other worthwhile ends. Each group, in order to secure support, must convince the total body of the value of its work. So at the most crucial moments in the life of the church, when personnel and money are being distributed, the church behaves more like a corporation with competing divisions than one body in Christ. Of course, if one stands far enough away, one can see that all programs are needed to provide a comprehensive ministry. But those on the scene do not enjoy that vantage point. They find themselves convincing the total body of the value of their own activity, and often competing with all the rest, all in the interest of the wholeness of the church!

In Chapter Six examples are given of workable ideas to help local churches plan programs for wholeness rather than for competition. Here it is useful to point out an intriguing method of local church planning that begins with an examination of the current cycle of Bible readings and allows those lessons to guide the congregation as it plans its life in worship, nurture, witness, and Bible study. For each season of the church year — Advent, Christmas, Epiphany, Lent, etc. — a planning team is formed. Each team, with representatives from each of the conventional committees, begins its work with a study of the lessons for that season, giving attention to the impact of those lessons on a congregation concerned about its responsibilities in the world. Thus the major activities of each season take shape under the control of scripture as understood by those responsible for guiding the church in its worship and learning, its witness and nurture. This approach is fully developed in *Social Themes of the Christian Year* edited by Dieter T. Hessel.[21]

The Fruits of Spirituality

The goal of traditional mysticism was easily expressed: the absorption of the self into the Divine. Progress toward this goal could be measured by religious exercises, days in solitude, years in the desert. But a spirituality for today will be measured not by quantitative means but by the quality and usefulness of our daily walk.

At this point we can turn to Meister Eckhart with greater appreciation. Eckhart used the biblical figures of Martha and Mary to illustrate spiritual maturity. Eckhart ranked Martha higher than Mary. He believed that Mary was still at school but that Martha had already learned her lesson.[22]

Spirituality should be tested by the "quality of our actions," says Mary McDermott Shideler. She notes:

> The books on spirituality and the spiritual guides tell us mostly of the heights and depths, but little of the daily-ness of life under the aspect of eternity. They warn us against succumbing to pride, envy, avarice, sloth, anger, gluttony, and lust, but rarely against the error of evaluating our spiritual state or status by the frequency and intensity of our "religious experiences."[23]

We began this chapter with a brief excursion into the history of the church to show how the Protestant Reformation encouraged the personal aspect of spirituality. We noted that John Calvin, in particular, avoided a spirituality that stressed union with the Divine. He was pointing away from the universal, toward the particular. Now let us acknowledge a spirituality that points away from the eternal, toward the temporal.

Shideler speaks for us again: "A notable mark of the spiritual person is that he translates his awareness of the ultimate into practical, everyday action, not only when he is all aglow but also when he is inwardly dull or darkened." Spirituality, as we now understand it, is ultimately pragmatic. "To act lovingly is more important than merely to feel affectionate. To treat particular persons and things as having an ultimate place and significance is more important than to be rapt in contemplation of a diffuse holiness investing in a generalized world." [24]

Recently a piano teacher died in Louisville, Kentucky. Described as a "local institution," James Garrison had taught some of the same students for many years. His teaching led students beyond technical skills to spiritual discovery. Garrison must have been a person who was able to translate his spirituality into meaningful daily living.

After the news of his death, two of his students, both adults, wrote letters to the Louisville *Courier-Journal* to share with the world what they had learned from Garrison. One, who had studied with him for nearly thirty years wrote, "We will miss his excitement for teaching us not only about piano, but also his love for life, God, and learning to stay young at heart."

Another former student, now a professor of English, testified that his first experience of "music's transcending power" came at the age of twelve when he heard one of Garrison's older students play Mendelssohn's G-minor concerto. The professor went on to say, "Dante said that when he saw Beatrice, all forms of enmity were banished in him, and he was filled with charity. Those of us privileged to work under Garrison have felt something similar — the power of harmony whose ultimate source in Garrison's life was the love of God." [25]

Spirituality seeking expression today is as much a way of being in the world as it is a way of being with God. The needs of the poor, the protection of the rights of minorities, freedom from sexual and political harassment, the quality of life for the elderly, a just and sustainable future, and the control of harmful substances are all issues for the spiritually mature. People who have met the God of the Bible seek a world where justice is as real as prayer. They insist upon and work for a society that is concerned with the fiber and not just the finish of life. Spirituality is demeaned when religious persons demand the appearance of religious symbols without structures to give them meaning.

The furor in many communities about the display of nativity scenes on public property is an example of this. Often the courts have had to resolve the dispute. Church groups have supported the displays of Christian symbols and claimed great victories when the displays have been allowed. Leaving aside the important matters of the rights of minorities and the use of public funds for sectarian purposes, what is "won" in such cases? Unless the government in all its structures and functions truly represents God revealed in Jesus Christ, how is Christ honored by a plaster figure on the courthouse lawn? Does a creche on the public square represent a victory, or does it represent the false prophet who cried "peace, peace," when peace did not exist?

Personal Spirituality and Relations with Others

Self-understanding grows from a personal relationship with God. Through prayer and meditation a person gains self-awareness as an object of God's love and grace. "Beloved, we are God's children now; it does not yet appear what we shall be . . ." (1 John 3:2). This awareness can develop whether the encounter with God is pleasant or painful.

For the writer of Psalm 27 the encounter with God was pleasant. It offered the psalmist protection and strength, and from that came the writer's self-understanding courage:

> The Lord is my light and my salvation;
> whom shall I fear?
> The Lord is the stronghold of my life;
> of whom shall I be afraid? (Psalm 27:1)

The awareness of God's protection gave the psalmist identity and personal strength.

But the person who feels alienated or estranged from God is also aware of her or his distinct self as a person in the presence of God:

> Lord, all my longing is known to thee,
> >   my sighing is not hidden from thee. . . .
> Do not forsake me, O Lord!
> >   O my God, be not far from me!
> Make haste to help me,
> >   O Lord, my salvation! (Psalm 38:9, 21-22)

Selfhood is affirmed when we are aware of God's presence, whether it comes from joy or anguish.

It is out of our relationship with God that selfhood develops, but it is out of our relationship with others that our self is given its shape. As we respond and react with other people, we discover our potential as creative and loving persons. The most basic forms of human interaction help us to know who we are and what we might become. "What is your name?" presents the issue of identity. "Have you lived here long?" introduces the issue of personal history. "What do you do?" asks about our personal mission and the matter of vocation.

Much misunderstanding comes from expecting too much from others. Our personal relationships can shape our spirituality, but they cannot create it. We are bound to be disappointed if we expect our friends to give what only God can provide. Those who expect orchids to grow from rose bushes are set up for disappointment and find it difficult to appreciate the rose when it appears.

When we are not satisfied with our deeper selves, we look to others in the mistaken hope that they can fill our inner void. So we move from friend to friend, spouse to spouse, mate to mate, always hoping that the next human relationship will fill the void that God alone can complete. This traffic in human personality is manipulation in its most advanced stage. We are expecting others to give us what only God can provide.

Spiritually mature people can appreciate the roses others bring to a relationship because orchids were never expected. They can celebrate the unique characteristics each person brings because those gifts enrich the common experience. Our ability to appreciate different perspectives, opinions, and values in others is a measure of our self-confidence, which does not depend on others but has come from God. Healthy spirituality results in personal relationships that are joyful and productive. When spiritually developed people come together, they rejoice in their differences and employ those differences as they work to reach common goals.

The late William Stringfellow embodied and witnessed to the kind of spirituality described in this chapter. In one of his last writings he said,

Being holy means a radical self-knowledge; a sense of who one is, a consciousness of one's identity so thorough that it is no longer confused with the identities of others, of persons or of any creatures or of God or of any idols.[26]

3

The Congregation Is the Place

Ed thumbed through the mail quickly. He had just enough time to drive from the church to the golf course to meet Bernie, moderator of the church board. Ed hoped there would be a good opportunity to visit with Bernie about a policy statement on ethical guidelines for the church's invested funds. The church should witness with its invested money as well as with its outreach offerings, or so Ed believed.

The only letter that looked important was one from the denominational district office. The address was hand-typed, so Ed thought it was personal. The letter was from the district minister. He was asking Ed to head a task force on spirituality for the district.

Like many denominational jobs, this was specific and well-defined. The task force was to study the needs of congregations and ways they serve the spiritual needs of their members. It was then to propose ways the district can help the congregations in their work. The task force "will report to the next district assembly and then be dissolved."

Ed left the letter on his desk and headed for the golf course. He was pleased that the denomination was giving attention to such an issue. *If the church doesn't do something about spirituality, then who will?* Ed thought.

But Ed realized that this was an issue different from those that churches usually deal with. Spirituality, as Ed understood it, was not a program such as education or outreach whose success could be measured by numbers or dollars. He believed spirituality was a way of doing what churches normally do. A "task force on

38

spirituality" was like a "task force on love" — a theological necessity but an administrative impossibility.

Ed said, "I'll do the job, but I think we'll have some interesting conversations before the job's done."

Guideline: *A congregation seeking to develop the spirituality of its members will not create a new program but will give fresh meaning to those already in place.*

Our understanding of Christian spirituality was born in the desert and grew up in the monastery. Before Christianity was a recognized religion, many believers left their homes to establish a solitary life of prayer in the desert, believing that this style of life was second only to death by martyrdom for those who would demonstrate faith. "It is with the image of spiritual combat that third-century men and women understood the need to go out into the desert to fight the demons and to find the angels. Both the demons and the angels were believed to live there in the desert." [27] These people were called "anchorites," from the Greek word that means *to withdraw.* "It was a life of continual meditation upon Scriptures and a time for strenuous training in order that one might ascend the ladder of perfection by the grace of God." [28]

Not all of these devout persons lived completely alone. Some spent a part of each day with others and developed a communal life of prayer. This was the beginning of the monastic life, which reached its peak with St. Benedict, who founded the monastery at Monte Cassino in 529. *The Rule of St. Benedict*, which governed Monte Cassino and the other monasteries that Benedict founded, set the pattern for spirituality. The influence of *The Rule* is still being felt; Benedict remains the single most important influence in English spirituality.

Those who seek a deeper life of the spirit today must still find a way to adjust to a spirituality whose shape was determined in the third century. Even today, retreats and pilgrimages remain the accepted paths to spirituality. While not questioning the value of the "retreat and withdraw" form of spirituality, we find it necessary to point out some limitations of a disciplined life that finds its roots in the desert and monastery.

The spirituality of retreat and withdrawal became part of a dualistic view of life that separated spirit from matter, good from evil, clergy from laity. Such dualism has been questioned at least since the time of the Renaissance and the Protestant Reformation. The Renaissance gave a new appreciation of the created order, and the Reformation struck a decisive blow at an ecclesiastical system that made people dependent upon the clergy for their salvation. In modern times the unity and interdependence of life has been affirmed by philosophers, scientists, and economists. Thus modern people seek to affirm the oneness of life in a world that has been created by God and redeemed by Jesus Christ.

As long as the desert retreat and the monastery are considered the only available locations for spiritual growth, anything less than a fully committed monastic life seems like a scaled-down version of the ideal. If real spirituality can only be discovered by a monk who has taken vows of poverty, chastity, and obedience, what significance can be attached to an annual weekend retreat? Commenting on the development of the monastery, church historian Williston Walker remarked that "the most unfortunate aspect of this double ideal was that it tended to discourage the efforts of the ordinary Christian."[29]

For most of the people who seek a deeper life of the spirit, retreat and withdrawal is simply not available. There are responsible parents, many without partners, who do not wish to leave their children for a weekend retreat. There are heads of households who work long hours, commute great distances, and often work on weekends. There are valuable citizens who give many hours of free time not only to religious groups but also to Boy Scouts, Girl Scouts, political parties, local action groups, peace organizations, and countless other worthwhile groups. Within each group can be found those who genuinely seek a richer life of the spirit. The desert and the monastery are not available to these people.

The Congregation As the Place

In place of the desert and the monastery let us consider the congregation as the focus for spirituality today. There are many reasons for this choice. First, a spirituality located within the congregation is not trapped in individualism. A congregation is concerned about marriages, births, graduations, ordinations, divorces, promotions, illnesses, firings, accidents, honors, and operations. Such a rich environment will nourish a spirituality that looks far beyond the individual.

A spirituality rooted in the congregation will also be enriched by a sense of place. Bred in the earth and located on a corner, a congregational spirituality may attain unmeasurable heights, but it will also reach out to those who need better housing and improved schools as well as those who destroy the earth and pollute the air and water in careless or deliberate ways.

Third, a spirituality nourished within a congregation knows its position in time. Congregations are aware of time because of what they hear and do. "In the beginning was the Word . . . In the year that King Uzziah died . . . When it was time for Mary to be delivered . . . And when the time had fully come . . . On the first day of the week . . . I am with you always, to the close of the age."

Having heard the Word, the congregation enacts the Word, allowing it to take on shape and form in the midst of the people. The place where the Word is heard and the sacraments are celebrated can become the place where persons can find ultimate meaning for their lives. The hearing and the enactment of the Word reveal the possibilities God has planted in each moment and in each place.

Congregations are something like gardens in early spring. The rich soil has been covered over by the dead leaves and dry reminders of the winter. But when the garden is raked, the bright-green shoots are discovered pushing themselves through the warm soil. That first sign of growth reminds the gardener of the purpose of the work and the joy that work provides.

The aim of this book is to restore the congregation as a place of meaning instead of activity only. And it is the aim of this specific chapter to suggest how the normal activities of the local church can be the occasion for spiritual encounter and growth. Let us turn to the ordinary tasks of the congregation and suggest the spiritual possibilities of each. In Chapter Six, we have provided some ways in which the ideas and possibilities can be realized in the actual programs of a local congregation.

The Congregation Orders Space

"Where is your church?" is the first question asked about a

congregation. That normal question implies that the church is a located institution requiring some relationship to the earth.

There were efforts in the late 1950s and the 1960s to establish "churches without walls." These efforts were a legitimate response to the post World War II building boom and its effect, "the suburban captivity of the church." Congregations responded by renting space in shopping centers and in other public places, not as interim sites but as permanent locations for worship. While these efforts helped church bodies see the spiritual risk in church establishment, the attempts to establish a worshiping community without a "holy" space were far from successful. Few of these experiments in theological idealism have survived.

Worshiping people are going to use space! It is an issue for an architect looking at an undeveloped lot and for the altar guild as it decides to replace the paraments. Since decisions about space usually survive the decision-makers, they should be carefully made.

There are two commandments to follow as the congregation orders space. The first is: *Keep it honest.* Any decision regarding the use of space must meet the standard of honesty. Because the God of truth is to be served, effects and atmosphere must yield to integrity and honesty. The house of worship must be a place where things *are* what they *appear* to be.

Professional planners can create different environments for the sake of variety and interest. Thus a hotel may have a "Victorian Room," a "Renaissance Room," and a "Williamsburg Room." Each room, however, is the same size and differs from the others only in wall treatment, floor covering, and lighting fixtures. No harm is done if conventions are held in the make-believe settings of hotel conference rooms.

But worship requires honesty! It is better for a church to have bare cinder blocks and a cross fashioned from a tree taken from the site than to worship in a room where synthetic materials have been manufactured to look like something else. A well-tuned piano is to be preferred over another instrument that pretends to be what it is not.

Every church, no matter the size, faces economic decisions. Churches large and small must shape their plans to fit the money available. At this point it is tempting to set honesty aside and choose the imitations and synthetics. For spiritual health it would be better to postpone the purchase or reduce the scope of the program. Honesty is as important a factor in economic decisions as it is in ethical decisions.

The second commandment regarding space is: *Keep it clean.* The piles of out-dated education materials, discarded furniture, costumes no longer worn, and unidentifiable photographs that clutter church buildings may not seem to be a hindrance to spiritual growth. But they bear silent witness that the institution is afraid to make the simplest of decisions and would rather cling to souvenirs of the past than face tomorrow's challenges. The Christian education committee of every local church needs to tour its own facilities, compare their appearance with those of the nearby school, and imagine the different feelings the same children experience as they move from school room to church school room.

The Congregation Orders Time

The Bible begins its story with the account of the Creator's daily work: "And there was evening and there was morning, a second day"(Genesis 1:8). The church continues to demonstrate responsibility for what happens in time.

The congregation recognizes time as it functions in the lives of its members. On a typical Sunday morning in the average church there will be a rosebud on the altar to announce the birth of a child, the "cherub choir" will sing, teenagers will serve as acolytes, a sixty-year-old will read the lessons, and the time and place of a funeral will be announced. These are ordinary events in congregational life, but their significance should be noted. The church is a multi-age community. It recognizes the gifts and challenges of every person at every stage of life.

Every distinct community has its own way of measuring time. The federal government points toward a budget year that begins in October. Some businesses operate on a fiscal calendar that begins the first of July. The school year begins in September. Some churches order time by beginning the year on the first Sunday in Advent. The church's distinctive ordering of time is a powerful learning tool, especially for young people. As youngsters observe the various seasons of the church year and notice how they coincide or fail to coincide with public events, they will learn in a subtle way what it means to be a Christian in a secular world. Chapter Six will offer concrete examples to show how the congregation can observe the church year in a meaningful and manageable way.

Sometimes the church can offer its own meaning to an event that has a purely secular origin. For the residents of the United States, the Sunday nearest Independence Day can be a time when the faithful reflect on the church's responsibility in a free society. It is an opportunity to show how the First Amendment to the Constitution can be used to strengthen the nation's life and institutions. While national policies receive thoughtful theological appraisal from the pulpit on the nation's birthday, hymns and anthems from the national composers can be offered in thanksgiving and praise.

Mother's Day, whose traditional celebration embarrasses and even angers many of today's mothers, offers the church an occasion to recognize the particular insights women have to share and to help church people understand the church's responsibility to the changing family and its values.

The Congregation Gathers for Rituals

The congregation provides a holy place for holy actions. For Christians, the central actions are baptism and holy communion. These acts constitute a congregation's primary avenue on the way to spiritual growth. Each of these sacred actions represents unlimited reservoirs of meaning that cannot be fully exhausted. Continual examination and reflection about baptism and the Lord's Supper keep their meanings fresh and lively.

The World Council of Churches has stimulated renewed interest in the sacramental discussion by printing its document *Baptism, Eucharist and Ministry*. Those who accuse the Council of supporting a distant coterie of out-of-touch executives, of a preference for third-world opinions in all matters, and the persistent promotion of revolutionary ideas may be surprised to discover the Council's statement on baptism to be so supportive of the local congregation. "Since baptism is intimately connected with the corporate life and worship of the Church, it should normally be administered during public worship, so that the members of the congregation may be reminded of their own baptism and may welcome into their fellowship those who are baptized and whom they are committed to nurture in the Christian faith."[30]

The World Council's statement enhances the role of the congregation as spiritual developer and moves the baptismal question beyond the impasse of infant versus believer's baptism. The new understanding of baptism can allow for either form because it sees baptism "as part of an ongoing process of Christian initiation and continuing growth in the Christian life."[31]

As the congregation is the location for baptism, it is also the site for the Lord's Supper. Participation in both of these celebrations assures us that our spiritual development will be grounded in time and space and related to the ongoing life of God's people. Regular appearance at the Lord's Table keeps us in contact with the authentic Christ rather than the Christ we might desire. Christ does not appear as a wandering philosopher or a whimsical teacher with fascinating stories. The Christ we meet at the table comes presenting the wounds of Calvary represented in bread and wine.

The spirituality developed at the Lord's Table identifies Christ for us and confirms our relationship with all of our brothers and sisters. The World Council statement stresses this: "The sharing in one bread and the common cup in a given place demonstrates and affects the oneness of the sharers with Christ and with their fellow sharers in all times and places. . . . Eucharistic celebrations always have to do with the whole Church, and the whole Church is involved in each local eucharistic celebration."[32]

Should there be any tendency for spirituality to be focused solely on the individual's intimate relationship with God, that tendency is reversed at the Lord's Table. "All kinds of injustice, racism, separation and lack of freedom are radically challenged when we share in the body and blood of Christ. Through the eucharist the all-renewing grace of God penetrates and restores human personality and dignity."[33]

Related to the rituals of baptism and the Lord's Supper are the acts of infant dedication and confirmation. Infant dedication takes place in churches where infants are not baptized. It gives the parents and the congregation the opportunity to thank God for the gift of new life, to share responsibility for the spiritual growth of the child, and to encourage the child to confess faith in Christ and be baptized as maturity develops. Confirmation is the completion of infant baptism and permits the young person to accept personal responsibility for her or his own spiritual growth.

A great deal of attention is being given by Christian educators and ecumenical leaders to these events. This interest has been stirred by new understandings of baptism and the Lord's Supper, by changing growth patterns of children, and by the acknowledgment of church people that western society is becoming increasingly secular.

John Westerhoff notes that "baptism, confirmation, and first communion have been placed in various orders to meet new situations. Each generation, in its social context has had to make a decision on how it will celebrate its faith and initiate persons into its life."[34] Westerhoff proposes baptism at birth, first communion in early childhood, a "Covenant of Discipleship" in early adolescence, and confirmation in adulthood. This sequence he calls "a faithful sequence for North American Christians in these times."

For churches who practice believers' baptism, a tension exists between the need to allow young people to receive communion at an age early enough so that they will not feel excluded from the Christian community and at the same time late enough so that they have the maturity to recognize the significance of the rite and the responsibilities that attend it. Some congregations may wish to develop a scheme in which the children of the church are given instruction regarding the Lord's Supper and allowed to partake regularly while postponing until early teen years a class in church membership culminating in baptism.

Although this sequence would allow communion to be received prior to one's baptism, it responds to the "social context" that Westerhoff mentions. More importantly, it allows the young person to prepare for church membership in a thorough fashion at an age when the other serious issues of life are being met.

The congregation may also consider ordering time in terms of the life-changing circumstances of its members. In addition to marriage, there are other events such as graduations and retirement that need to be recognized in the context of the worshiping community. They bring profound changes in the way people relate to church and society.

The most significant "rite of passage" in American life takes place when the young person is given a driver's license. It represents entry into the world of adult action and responsibility. If a congregation were to recognize this moment in the life of each of its young people, each person would be reminded in a positive way of the responsibilities of citizenship. Concern about the use of alcohol and drugs would be presented in the context of Christian decision-making.

The most controversial ordering of time is provided by acts of worship taking place at the time of a divorce. Such a ritual has been provided by the book of worship of the United Church of Christ and by others as well. This act of worship provides a way for the divorcing partners to say in the words of the liturgy what they are not as yet prepared to say in their own words. It provides the first steps in the healing process, and it allows the church to offer its support when people need it most.

In recent years our society has increased its understanding of the needs people have when they retire. Most corporations develop a pre-retirement program for each employee so that the final weeks on the job will be fruitful and pleasant. Long before the retirement party takes place, the company has helped the employee anticipate the social, financial, and psychological changes that are coming. In addition, communities of all sizes provide organizations that offer recreation, entertainment, service, and the chance to learn new hobbies and skills.

Many churches serve retired people in similar ways. Fewer, however, are the local congregations where the spiritual needs of the retired person are discovered, studied, and served. Most church programs provided for retired people seem designed to keep people busy — too busy, perhaps, to allow them to think and reflect. "I'm busier now than I was when I was working" is a frequent observation of the newly-retired. If the corporation and the community are serving the psychological and social needs of the older adult, the church is free to address the spiritual needs. Congregations can provide the comfortable social structure and the spiritual counsel to help older people prepare for and face death. A thoughtful congregation will give retired people an opportunity to reflect as well as stay busy.

Congregations can also help people deal with one of the most difficult of problems — the disposition of earthly remains. Many congregations are developing a garden where the cremated remains of church members are buried in a place of quiet beauty undisturbed by urns, stones, or markers. Modest fees charged provide enough funds to maintain the garden. Such facilities, carefully located on church grounds, are providing people with an accessible alternative to other forms of burial.

Other congregations are providing crypts for the disposition of cremated remains. Unlike the memorial garden, this arrangement provides a particular location for each person.

When a congregation decides to provide a place for the cremated remains of members, it should be careful not to offend the sensibilities of those who prefer more traditional burial practices. As burial costs rise and more churches offer their property for the disposition of cremated remains, the acceptance of this method will increase.

The Congregation Articulates the Faith

People who know churches may sometimes wonder if anything good can come from such a Nazareth — especially the gospel! The gathered community seems more like driftwood washed ashore during last night's storm than a great tree that has grown and thrived through many storms and sunrises. Crying babies, whispering teenagers, disappointed wives, unfaithful husbands, recovering alcoholics, and victims of Alzheimer's Disease gather in their customary places to hear the customary preacher. The preacher is a further witness for the absurd. The preacher's assignment is first to hear the gospel. But often the sound of the gospel is muted by the noise created by personal problems, professional desires, occupational burnout, and intellectual weariness. But if the gospel has been heard, it must then be fashioned so it will be grasped by hearers who are more accustomed to being a passive audience than a responsive congregation.

The apostle said, "We have this treasure in earthen vessels" (2 Corinthians 4:7). In whatever ways are appropriate, each congregation should find a way to display the treasure. The congregation provides the occasion for the gospel to be announced and received. But that process is not limited to the act of preaching and hearing. The sermon does not end in the pulpit but continues as people gather in other places to question, to "try on" what they have heard, and to challenge the preacher's vision. In such a situation, the preacher is driven to probe deeper into the heart of the gospel, and the hearers discover that the gospel is a sharing as well as a hearing.

Exciting things happen when the congregation joins the pastor in Bible study in preparation for sermon writing. The people and the pastor may study the recommended lessons several weeks ahead of the scheduled use. The group will use commentaries and other resources to learn the how, when, and where of the passages being studied. Equally important will be the contribution of each person present as the members share their personal response to the Scriptures.

At least four positive developments come from this common study. First, people will read the Bible seriously, and their reading will often come from portions of the Bible that have been ignored. Second, people grow closer to one another as they take part in intentional, purposeful Bible study. Third, the pastor is able to construct a sermon based upon the serious grappling of lay people with the text. Fourth, sermons grown in such a setting are listened to eagerly and acutely.

Sermons written as a result of such a process are no longer the preacher's burden. They are more accurately described as the articulation of the people's faith. They provide an opportunity for the people to hear and respond to God's word, which they have already encountered in group study and prayer.

The Congregation Orders Its Life

A congregation's spiritual agenda must be discovered in its organizational life. Spirituality is not something that can be assigned to a subcommittee of the worship department. It should inform all aspects of the church's life. The spiritual goals of the entire congregation should be clearly in focus when the congregation identifies, recruits, and trains its leaders. A congregation growing in spirituality will develop leaders who have a vision of the congregation's total life.

For the sake of efficiency, congregations often match leaders with positions that match their daily work. Thus the contractor is asked to head the property committee, the bank officer becomes the church treasurer, and the school principal is nominated to lead the Christian education program. But church leadership requires more than a transfer of skills from the marketplace to the church. Even people who are qualified by daily work to perform certain duties should be supported by a comprehensive understanding of and commitment to the total mission of the church. Spirituality can inform all phases of the congregation's life. Spiritually developed leaders share their vision of the whole church, even though they may be engaged in a sharply defined area of church life.

As each group within the church begins its annual work, it should define the spiritual dimensions of its responsibilities. This is not to suggest the use of pious language to define mundane activities but to probe beneath the operational guidelines for the spiritual foundations of each committee's work. Here are some suggestive definitions of typical church groups:

Property Committee: The work of this department will create the physical environment that will enhance the church's growth in worship, education, and fellowship. As it does its work, this committee will seek to preserve the natural environment and respect the natural properties of the church's building materials.

Evangelism Committee: The work of this committee will enable people to hear and respond to the call of Christ in their own lives and respond by uniting with the church and observing the social consequences of that call.

Membership Committee: This committee will seek ways to demonstrate Christ's concern to every member of the congregation, giving special attention to the homebound, the sick, the mourning, the elderly, and the disabled.

Outreach Committee: This department will seek to extend the love and mercy of Christ to all individuals and groups.

Worship Committee: The Worship Committee will enable the congregation to develop a vital relationship to God through Jesus Christ in both corporate and private worship.

Christian Education Committee: This department will provide opportunities for people to grow in the Christian faith so that they may be informed and equipped to witness in their daily life.

The congregation's greatest opportunity for spiritual growth develops in the countless meetings of boards, committees, task forces, and other groups formed to do the church's work. Since the typical congregation schedules more meetings than it does services of worship, it should recognize the spiritual promises of each business meeting.

In the way that churches have separated spiritual development from church business, they have maintained the dualism of soul and body that has distorted the faith throughout the centuries. A church executive makes this observation: "Most boards, committees, and task forces do their business in a secular rather than a spiritual way. It is as if the church has relegated spirituality to the pastoral realm of the church's life and assumed that successful church administration must be exclusively pragmatic in its focus."[35]

Church business meetings can allow the resources of the Bible, prayer, silence, and reflection to influence the work at hand. Scripture lessons can be carefully selected to direct the group to the agenda before them. A time for silent meditation may follow. This allows members to reflect on what has just been heard and helps prepare for greater participation. "Times of silence are modest but very important times of surrender that allow us to wait upon God in the expectation that we will be acted upon in some way. When we are silent before a church meeting, the sharp edges of the agenda are removed."[36]

A prayer before a meeting, if not offered in a perfunctory way, allows God to make a community out of individuals who have hurriedly arrived from many different places and diverse duties. It can have profound effects on a meeting. "An invitation that asks God to empower a board to arrive at a common mind about a thorny issue can inspire the group to avoid power struggles and I-win-you-lose decisions." At the conclusion of the meeting the group can take part in some reflection on the meeting, commenting on the helpful things that took place.[37]

Within every congregation are gifted people who are burned out and used up. They still worship and contribute their money but have a ready refusal when the nominating committee calls. They turn down further service because church work has depleted their spiritual resources. A pastor observes, "Church life consists of a demanding round of extroverted activities that often leave our people exhausted in body and hungry in spirit. . . . What I hear more frequently from some of our best church members is this: 'It seems like I'm giving out and giving out all the time with not much coming back. I don't need another job; I need nurture.'"[38]

A prayer of the church asks "that our work may not be in us a burden but a delight." When the normal life of the parish becomes spiritually fulfilling, people will welcome leadership positions for the growth and strength they will receive.

The Congregation Nurtures Its Members

The programs and activities of the church that are usually classified as Christian education can play a significant role in encouraging the spiritual growth of church members. Previous sections of this chapter have uncovered the possibilities of educational enterprises such as the membership class and the lectionary study group. The traditional Christian education opportunities, such as Sunday school classes, Bible study groups, and vacation church school sessions can all be places where spirituality is offered to children, young people, and adults.

A basic and important approach is to include spirituality issues as a content area in Christian education events and in curriculum. To be sure, studying spirituality is not the same as having a spiritual experience. An intellectual approach is not being offered as a substitute for a direct relationship with God. But it should be acknowledged that part of the hunger for spiritual growth comes from a longing for clarity, a desire to understand just what is meant by prayer and meditation and other terms associated with the spiritual life. Offering spirituality as a content area may not lead all students to seek a more disciplined spiritual life, but removing some of the mystique is an appropriate goal. Further, the study of spirituality will remove some of the barriers that keep people from acknowledging their own spiritual needs.

Teachers and planners should take care to ensure that the material chosen is age-appropriate. For example, the details of Julian of Norwich's visions of Christ might be too graphic for an elementary class! But there will be no shortage of available material for any age group. Prepared Sunday school curricula are providing more content about spirituality in response to the growing interest. All students would benefit from a study of the classical spiritual disciplines of prayer, fasting, Bible study, and meditation. Autobiographies, in book form or through audiovisual presentations, of people who developed strong spiritual lives may be helpful.

Theology is a subject generally studied only in seminaries, but its absence in our church schools is partially responsible for our spiritual crisis. Surely the church school class is the place where students could study basic theological concepts such as sin, grace, and forgiveness. A prepared teacher could employ the biblical material and theological resources to make these concepts accessible to church members. Too often lay people have been left with the idea that spirituality is for the clergy. If no steps are taken to make the material of spirituality understood by all, such a disastrous misconception will go unchallenged.

Besides providing opportunities for encountering spirituality as a subject matter to be explored and understood, Christian education programs can also be the place where spirituality is experienced. In any number of settings, students can learn to pray, to meditate, and to read the Bible in a nonthreatening environment. Classes for children and young people are especially good places, because most young people have not yet developed the fear of prayer that some adults have. If children could be taught that prayer is a natural part of life, they will be more likely to use prayer as an aid in their own spiritual lives.

Teaching spirituality as a subject area and as an experience is a responsibility some teachers may view as overwhelming. Teachers will need special training and preparation in order to feel comfortable in the area of spiritual growth. Further, they may want to be offered retreats or workshops where they can be spiritually nurtured. A congregation attempting to encourage spiritual growth through Christian education should pay special attention to the needs of its teachers.

The Congregation Links Members to the World

The phrase "local church" describes the tension in which each congregation is called to live. Because it is local, the congregation speaks with a familiar accent that is understandable to its neighbors. The building is constructed of local materials according to the plans of a local architect. Its soup kitchen may serve a few who are "just passing through," but most of its clients are regulars, part of the neighborhood.

Because it is "church," its concerns are not limited to the local. Thus the congregation is as committed to the hungry and homeless around the world as to those in its immediate neighborhood. Difference in location, culture, and political loyalties do not reduce the church's concern for others but rather describe the conditions in which the church must witness.

In a society where individualism is promoted, the church is one of the few places where concern for the world is valued above self-interest. Spirituality nurtured in a congregation is more than private. It relates first to the church community and then to the world. By keeping a concern for spirituality in mind, the congregation's links to the world will be stronger.

4

Partnerships for a New Era

Everyone called her "Ms. Moneybags" because Ellen had been church treasurer for so many years. Each month the board looked forward to her carefully prepared financial reports—every cent of income duly acknowledged, every expenditure accurately reported. Her nickname was one of the ways the church showed its appreciation for Ellen's faithful service. The leaders knew it was not easy to balance the books of a stable congregation with an old building in a time of lay-offs and early retirements.

So the board members were shocked when Ellen's report showed not the usual modest balance but a surplus of seven thousand dollars. Not even the old-timers could remember when the monthly statement looked so healthy.

"Our strong balance," Ellen explained, "is due to an undesignated gift of five thousand dollars from an anonymous church member."

Many ways were suggested to solve the unusual problem of surplus money! A scholarship for church campers, a contribution to the nearby church college, a reserve for unexpected expenditures, a new seal for the church parking lot, and a gift to the pastor's seminary were all considered.

But two other ideas enjoyed more support than the rest. The board had already heard that the community's food pantry was closing due to government cutbacks. Members also heard that the new chapel needed drapes and a carpet before it could be dedicated. The chapel would be open twenty-four hours a day and available to all.

The moderator suggested that the worship committee chairperson meet with the social ministries chairperson and present a recommendation at next month's meeting.

Guideline: *A congregation seeking to develop the spirituality of its members will encourage the development of prayer and study as well as programs for social justice, for both are essential to spiritual growth.*

In the past decade, two kinds of movements have shown vitality and have gained in popularity throughout most denominations in the United States. One can be loosely termed "charismatic" or "evangelical." People attracted to the charismatic groups within their congregation or denomination are those who crave a more active spiritual life, people who believe that what is missing in the church is an energizing sense of the presence of God. These groups may be theologically diverse, but they all seek personal and corporate experiences that are more enlivened by the Holy Spirit.

The second movement that has had an impact on all churches could be called the "social action" movement. While never dead (as is also the case with the charismatic movement), the social action movement experienced a rebirth in the 1980s when issues such as disarmament, Central America, federal spending cuts, and apartheid begged to be addressed in the churches. Social activists are concerned that their churches speak out on issues, embody biblical values rather than cultural values, and encourage their members to give of their time and money to making changes in society.

Anyone who has been a part of a congregation knows of the dangers when these two groups drift too far apart from one another. The charismatics can become so concerned with individual experience that they lose sight of the mission of the church. Social activists often get caught up in time-consuming projects that lead them either to forget about the other important roles of the church or to become so tired and disenchanted, they leave the church. "Activists are accused of forsaking their souls for a cause, and pietists are ridiculed for sticking their heads in the sand as the world falls apart."[39]

On the other hand, groups that have been able to merge these two vital concerns are known for their powerful witness. One well-known example is the Sojourners community in Washington, D.C. Sojourners is a community grounded in prayer and Bible study, actively involved in local programs to aid the homeless and in peace education projects. Sojourners also is the founder of Witness for Peace, providing a continuous presence along the Nicaragua-Honduras border.

Not every local congregation is called to imitate the Sojourners model, for each church must be faithful to its unique situation. But it seems clear that the church will only be internally strong and able to witness to the world when the concerns of both the charismatics and the social activists are adequately addressed.

Abundant examples of the union of spirituality and social action can be found in the Bible. Mary Cosby describes the call of Moses in such a way. After the burning bush experience, Moses saw the suffering of the slaves in Egypt through God's eyes. He led the Hebrew people out of slavery, not in blind obedience to God, but passionately, because of the new awareness he had been given.[40]

This same newness of vision was a gift given to the Hebrew prophets, though it was often reluctantly received. Their call for a return to God was simultaneously a call to justice, to better treatment of the widows and the poor, and to more fitting lifestyles.

In the Gospels we find Jesus concerned about the wholeness of human life. His healing of a physical ailment was done never for show but as a step toward returning the ill person to full human living. Through his parables and by his example, he threw out the prejudices of his day, disregarding them as unacceptable in life lived under a new reign. His own ministry to the hurting was fueled by time spent in prayer. The biblical witness is a reminder of the strength that can be found when spirituality and social concern are wed.

If a church cannot find a way to merge the concerns for spirituality and social justice, it risks losing credibility in light of the biblical tradition. It also risks losing strength and vitality. And if the church does not keep a proper balance between concern for itself and concern for the world, it faces another risk. This risk, seldom mentioned, is that good people, who care about the world, will leave the church when they perceive it to be ineffective in responding to the needs of the world.

Two remarkable twentieth-century American Christians, William Stringfellow and Dorothy Day, are mentors to many who attempt to make their own lives whole. Both came close to abandoning the church because of its inadequacies. William

Stringfellow was an attorney, lecturer, activist, and author who was able to combine a deep spirituality with political activism. But his early experiences could have easily discouraged his interest in the church. Especially profound are his memories of how the Holy Spirit was misrepresented: "In my experience as a child in the church, when adults named the Holy Spirit in the presence of children it was always an utterly obscure, unspecified, literally spooky allusion."[41] Stringfellow contrasts this early experience with his later Bible studies, in which he says, "I found the Bible to be definitive and lucid as to the identity, character, style, and habitat of the Holy Spirit. . . . Biblically, the Holy Spirit means the militant presence of the Word of God . . . in . . . creation."[42] The discovery that the Holy Spirit was not a possession of the church was liberating to Stringfellow.

It is difficult to find a contemporary life that better combined authentic spirituality with social action than that of Dorothy Day. Day, the Roman Catholic woman who founded the Catholic Worker houses, is often described as the one person most responsible for the revitalization of the Catholic church in the United States in recent decades. Yet for nearly sixteen years in her early adulthood, Dorothy Day did not worship in a church nor participate in any form of organized religion. As a child, her experiences with the church were not unpleasant, and awakened in her a religious sensibility. As she also became politically aware in her later teens, though, she came to see conflicts between the church and the world. Specifically, she was troubled that the church was preaching of the "world beyond," rather than concerning itself with the problems of the world at hand.[43] Fortunately for both the church and the world, Day was called back into the church, both by experiences in her brief marriage and by her encounter with Peter Maurin.

Certainly congregations are interested in being places where spirituality and social concern grow together. We desire such a union because it is theologically sound and appropriate to our biblical witness. No church should attempt such an endeavor simply to attract the right kind of member. But it is well to remember the disillusionment of William Stringfellow and Dorothy Day. And it is exciting to imagine the kinds of members our churches can nurture in the future if they can offer a union of spirituality and social concern.

Authentic Spirituality Leads to Social Action

Earlier in this book, we defined spirituality as an attitude toward life or a way of being in the world. This definition implies that spirituality has to do with the whole of one's life. It is more than feeling, and it is more than thinking about God. In this chapter we have given content to our definition, by stating that our way of being in the world is grounded in the biblical tradition. A biblically-based spirituality cannot, by definition, be merely a good feeling or good thoughts. As our previous biblical examples indicate, true spirituality always leads outward, in concern about the other. But how does this movement outward take place?

A mature spirituality, before moving one outward, first helps people to enlarge their vision of the world. Catholic theologian Matthew Fox defines spirituality as "compassion." Compassion, he says, has to do with recognizing the interconnections that exist between all of creation. For Fox, spirituality is a compassionate attitude toward all of life.[44] Sensing the interconnectedness of all of creation will give a person a passionate desire to change or save creation. Such a foundation is a stronger impetus for social action than the belief, "I want to do it because it's right." Compassion moves beyond sympathy to empathy.

In a more practical way, it is to be hoped that taking up one of the traditional spiritual disciplines, such as prayer, meditation, or Bible study, would automatically lead a person or a group toward meaningful social action. Experience proves, however, that this is not always the case. Care must be taken to set appropriate goals for spiritual disciplines. For example, an appropriate goal for a Bible study on Paul's letter to the Romans might be: to understand the situation Paul was addressing, to see what the biblical tradition has to say to *our* contemporary situation, and to discuss what changes would need to take place in our lives or in our church to make us more responsive to the word of God. Such a Bible study would set the stage for action. On the other hand, an inappropriate goal would end with understanding the biblical situation.

In order for spirituality to lead to social action, the spiritual disciplines chosen must be undertaken with thoughtful preparation. When approached with care, many of the resources of the church can be used to lead the members to spiritual growth and to social responsibility. John Westerhoff describes such a process: "A renewed concentration on Jesus Christ will provide us with a common ground for judging and inspiring our lives. . . . A church that is faithful to Jesus Christ will be closer to God and at the same time closer to humanity: in uniting religious experience with prophetic action the church becomes more Christian."[45]

The notion that there is a direct relationship between spirituality and social transformation is by no means a solely contemporary idea. Two historical examples point to different ways in which spiritual growth leads to social action. Meister Eckhart, the German mystic, was very clear about the implications that his theology and spirituality had for social and political action: "We should abandon raptures sometimes for the sake of a better love which is to perform a loving ministry of work where it is most needed, whether spiritually or physically. . . . I consider it far better that you leave your rapture out of love and serve the needy person with what is a bigger love by far."[46] For Eckhart, there is no distinction between spiritual service and the social or physical needs of persons. The mystical believer cannot live in a world of fantasy, pretending that heaven is on earth. The mystic must live in recognition of the present reality: the fact that there is hell on earth. Matthew Fox writes about of Eckhart's beliefs: "It is this hell, this not-yet, this chasm between heaven and earth that drives the mystical believer into prophetic action and consciousness."[47]

Catherine of Siena, a fourteenth-century Italian mystic, wrote several hundred letters in her lifetime that explain the ways in which she saw her faith relating to the world around her. In particular, she called for more justice in the treatment of the poor, and she attacked the institutional corruption she saw displayed in the social, political, and religious organizations of her day. She demanded that Christians act in accordance with their beliefs. Divine justice makes no sense, Catherine said, if Christians do not respond to each other with acts of justice. Further, those who do acts of injustice harm themselves spiritually. Two observations she made about an unjust lawyer clarify her feelings: "He despises virtue who has a duty to perform for his neighbor and does not render that service unless he sees some personal advantage for himself. . . . He is cruel toward his own soul because he offends the poor."[48]

Meister Eckhart and Catherine of Siena both describe how spiritual maturity and direct engagement with the poor are interre-

60

lated. The relationship between spirituality and social transformation takes on a more explicitly political form in the thought of contemporary Latin American theologian Gustavo Gutierrez. Gutierrez believes that to place oneself in the perspective of the Kingdom (or the Reign of God) means to participate in the struggle for the liberation of the oppressed. Conversion, for Gutierrez, is a constant process that entails conversion to the Lord *and* conversion to the neighbor. This conversion is a radical transformation of ourselves, and accordingly we are committed to the radical transformation of the world around us.

Gutierrez recognizes the fact that a Christianity lived in commitment to the process of liberation presents many problems and obstacles. He says, however, that if this Christianity, this liberation, is rooted in an intense and concrete spirituality, those obstacles can always be overcome by one's encounter with God. This is not sentimental spirituality; he is not trying to appease people or win them over to his side. Rather, he is calling for a new understanding of spirituality that will more directly relate to the contemporary situation:

> A spirituality is a concrete manner, inspired by the Spirit, of living the Gospel; it is a definite way of living "before the Lord," in solidarity with all men, "with the Lord," and before men. . . . This is a spirituality which dares to sink roots into the soil of oppression — liberation.[49]

For Gutierrez, spirituality is inseparable from political action or social transformation. This was also the opinion of Thomas Merton, who lived out his views in a different way than most of the liberation theologians recommend. Merton wrote a great deal about monasticism, but most of his writing can be applied to Christians in general. Throughout his writings, Merton discards the monastic stereotype of rejecting the world. The contemplative, as any Christian, has a responsibility to live fully in the present situation. Merton says that rejection of the world is not a choice but is the evasion of choice. The choice *is* to choose the world:

> To choose the world is not then merely a pious admission that the world is acceptable because it comes from the hand of God. It is first of all an acceptance of a task and a vocation in the world, in history and in time. In any time, which is the present. To choose the world is to choose to do the work I am capable of doing, in collaboration with

my brother, to make the world better, more free, more just, more livable, more human.[50]

For Merton, true spirituality always and necessarily involves confrontation with the world, and the struggle to right the wrongs found in the world. True spirituality is radical confrontation with God: it is plumbing the depths. After such a relationship with God, and in the midst of such relationship, one's reaction to the world can never be the same. Apathy or complacency are no longer possible. Merton argues for the need in the world for prayer and meditation, which is the monk's vocation. His words are relevant for all Christians:

> This is an age that, by its very nature as a time of crisis, of revolution, of struggle, calls for the special searching and questioning which are the work of the monk in his meditation and prayer. . . . In reality the monk abandons the world only in order to listen more intently to the deepest and most neglected voices that proceed from its inner depth.[51]

We have described how spiritual growth can lead to social action, and we have read how spirituality is enriched by meaningful activity. It is also true that social action learns from spirituality. Those people who have committed their lives to working on causes that promote peace and justice find their work frustrating and empty when they are not spiritually fed. A deep spiritual life gives a person a vision of the world as it could be. This vision sustains people through temporary setbacks and difficult situations:

> A good example of how this can happen occurred when one family was involved in a church group that was renovating some substandard housing. Each Saturday when the crew assembled, the pastor would gather the workers for a brief discussion of why they were there. The vision was that every resident of the District of Columbia would have adequate housing. Their piece of that vision was to rehabilitate one section of the city. Reflecting on that vision with others made the grime and cockroaches more bearable, and it bound them together as a group.[52]

A strong spiritual life can have the effect of empowering and energizing a person; it can make one able to concentrate more and work more effectively. These attributes are all coveted by those who undertake the difficult work on behalf of the poor. Dorothy

Day found a personal spiritual life essential, and she nurtured it with daily mass and other disciplines, and with occasional spiritual retreats marked by rigor and austerity. She testified to the impact of the retreats upon her life:

> It is not only for others that I must have these retreats. It is because I too am hungry and thirsty for the bread of the strong. I too must nourish myself to do the work I have undertaken; I too must drink at these good springs so that I may not be an empty cistern and unable to help others.[53].

A journalist who visited Dorothy Day during her eightieth year found her spirituality to be a remarkable aspect of her life, which she took for granted:

> It appears that her strength is rooted in her spirituality. To rise at 6 each morning and spend 2 hours reading the Bible, meditating, and praying is as natural to her as eating breakfast. She mentions it only incidentally, after you pointedly ask. But the influences of this contemplative life are transparent.[54]

The problems of contemporary society are complicated, and working toward solutions requires patience, energy, and commitment. Developing a strong personal spirituality and being part of a faith community that fosters spiritual growth helps individuals enormously by increasing their stamina and keeping alive their vision. Finally, a deep spirituality can bring people closer to Jesus, who in his own life combined spirituality and active concern for others:

> If social ministries happen in this faith framework, the passion and intensity will deepen rather than burn out — or burn us out. The secret is in the marriage of the inner journey to an outward expression of this new inwardness in costly service to the victims of our time. The passion is fueled by the passion of Jesus. We no more burn out than he burned out, for we are in touch with the source of life and in touch with our own deepest being.[55]

What Do We Mean by Social Action? The Changing Role of Outreach

Most congregations have committees or departments with titles such as "World Outreach Committee," "Community Service

Committee," or "Missions Department." The role of such a committee is to make the congregation aware of the needs of the world and help the congregation to respond. Generally such committees are responsible for allocating a portion of the church budget, deciding which denominational, local, and other groups are most deserving of that church's money. People on the outreach committee expend a great deal of energy each year convincing the finance department that the outreach apportionment needs to be larger. They might also find it necessary to plead the outreach case each month as the treasurer decides which bills to pay. Some committees also encourage the congregation to study the needs of the world and to actually participate in various projects. The outreach committee is responsible for helping the local church to maintain its integrity and sense of purpose. Because of congregational support, denominational and ecumenical agencies have been able to make noticeable steps in defeating the forces of poverty and injustice over the past century.

As we look toward the twenty-first century, however, we might consider changes churches can make in the way they perceive their social responsibility. First, social responsibility in our present era requires that we be concerned with changing living conditions not only in other places but also in our own lifestyles. The very words *outreach* and *mission* imply the need to change and help the *other*. Responsible Christians in the waning years of the twentieth century would do well to broaden the spectrum of the mission of the church. In addition to concern for the poor and the disenfranchised, the question of our own lifestyles must be raised. The congregation can be the place where crucial and difficult issues regarding our responsibility for the problems of the world are raised.

It is well-known and well-documented that the first world is depleting the planet's resources at an alarming rate. We are aware that the majority of us North Americans are wealthier than we need to be, and most of us have no ability to discern between our "needs" and our "wants." We are not surprised to learn that many of our goods are produced by third-world citizens who are paid less in a year than many of us make in a week. These facts are known by many, but they are scarcely spoken of in church. Certainly the congregation could be the place, should be the place, where such delicate and important issues are raised.

A congregation concerned about the spiritual health of its

members risks losing its integrity if such issues are *not* discussed, in fact. For authentic spirituality is a *truthful* way of looking at the world. Only if we can see that we stand in need of transformation as much as do those in other parts of the world will we be articulating the mission of the church for the contemporary world. So, a socially responsible congregation will look at itself with new eyes, eyes intent to see our lifestyles for what they really are, eyes awaiting the vision of how we might change.

A socially responsible congregation will also look at the world differently. The world we were called to care for in Genesis has changed drastically in the past several decades. Not only are we responsible for the poor, the homeless, and the prisoner; we must also be responsible for the health of the planet itself, and indeed for the future. We are living in what has been called the "ecological, nuclear age." As people for the first time aware of the disastrous effect our living has had on the planet, and as the first generation to live with the threat of a nuclear holocaust, we must be responsive. Furthermore, we, in particular, are called to be responsive simply because we *can* be:

> As mainstream, middle-class Christians we have the leisure and the power to attend to these basic but semiremote threats to life as our sisters and brothers oppressed by more immediate and daily threats to survival do not.[56]

This responsibility may seem like a heavy burden, but it may be welcomed by many in individual congregations. Despite a vocal minority of church leaders who claim to be overworked, there are many people who are hungry for meaningful ways to spend their free time. Active men and women in early retirement are valuable resources for churches called to channel people's time and energy toward important projects. The stewardship of human talent is a challenge the church can joyfully accept as it strives to minister to a complicated and hurting world.

Congregations concerned with both spirituality and social action may have not only letters from African missionaries pinned on their bulletin boards but also charts explaining the ozone layer. Speakers on Mission Sunday need not only discuss the work of the local food pantry but also how our own diets can be changed to reflect greater responsibility. The mission field has expanded. The church lives in an ecological, nuclear age not by claiming to have the answers that our scientists and politicians search for, but by responding to this new age with greater understanding, new sensitivity, and a willingness to change.

Perhaps the church's role in such dangerous times is to be the place where people come, not to escape the problems of the world, but to face them with courage and wisdom. By constantly holding forth God's vision of the world, the church can empower people to do all they can to make that vision reality. Thomas Merton states the purpose of the church in this way:

> One of our most important tasks today is to clear the atmosphere so that men can understand their plight without hatred, without fury, without desperation, and with the minimum of goodwill. A humble and objective seriousness is necessary for the long task of restoring mutual confidence and preparing the way for the necessary work of collaboration in building world peace. This restoration of a climate of relative sanity is perhaps more important than specific decisions regarding the morality of this or that strategy, this or that pragmatic policy.[57]

What Can One Church Do?

With such an expanded view of the world, we may find the task of responding to its needs overwhelming. A logical and understandable question is: "Is there anything one congregation can do that will make a difference?" There are at least two areas in which the local congregation *can* make a difference, areas that can be approached by taking small yet meaningful steps. The two areas are lifestyle and community.

As mentioned earlier, in order to be truthful, the church must not ignore the problems of the average North American lifestyle. Naming the facts and creating an awareness of the effects of our living is one step. Taken by itself, however, that one step will most likely lead to anger, frustration, and apathy.

Providing alternatives to the average lifestyle is the creative and challenging second step. Leaders of congregations, both lay and clergy, usually face the second step with fear and trembling. Such apprehension is natural. After all, when we discuss people's lifestyles, we are discussing the most personal choices that people make. Further, leaders are often afraid to bring up lifestyle issues for fear that their own ways of living will be scrutinized, leaving them open to the charge of hypocrisy.

Non-threatening approaches are available, however. A study group could read the literature on simple living and alternative lifestyles. The youth group could prepare a meal consisting entirely of garden-raised produce. The women's fellowship could start a children's clothing exchange, providing a fun alternative to buying new and expensive clothes each season.

Although some people will undoubtedly be resistant, once the topic has been introduced in church, generally, the reactions are most favorable. For most of us are uncomfortable with our life-styles; we just do not know what choices we have. Many people welcome knowing about alternatives.

An area especially ripe for change is Christmas. All of us moan when Christmas catalogs arrive in August. None of us like the commercialization of this holiday. We know we spend too much money, we eat too much, and we find Advent full of anxiety and hurry. Yet where are the alternatives? The church can make resources available to people on how to make Christmas meaning-ful again. Family rituals can be taught and shared. Workshops on making Advent wreaths and calendars are themselves simple celebrations.[58]

Many men and women who have already been aware of the need for lifestyle changes have been reluctant to make the desired adjustments. It is difficult to stand against the attractions of our consumer society; it is almost impossible to take such a stand alone. With the support of their church, however, many people may have the encouragement they need to begin the move towards simpler living.

Supporting people as they appraise needed changes in their lives is one way the church functions as a community. As we have discussed earlier, congregations seeking to nurture the spiritual development of their members should take seriously the conditions under which most people live. One condition of modern life, noted by many observers, is the disintegration of community and com-munities. In our mobile society, few people live close to members of their extended family. Divorce has occasioned a new meaning to the word *family*. Small towns are losing residents, urban neighbor-hoods are rapidly changing. In sum, the communities that provided support and a sense of belonging to our grandparents at the beginning of this century rarely exist today. Yet the need for community is as compelling as ever.

Basically, people need to know that others care about them. When an individual discovers a caring community, this basic need is met. But a caring community can do far more than produce good, warm feelings. Being a part of a community gives hope to one's life. Facing personal and global problems is easier, because the community has given a glimpse of the future as it could be. In other words, a community can give people impetus to want to change the world because they feel better about the possibilities of the future.

A congregation can become a community, a place where members are encouraged to care about one another (and thus, the world) in a fulfilling way. Some congregations are now communities for many of their members. Professor of preaching Ronald J. Allen has suggested that one way to move toward community is to replace the word *fellowship* with the word *partnership*. Allen notes that the Greek word *koinonia*, which appears throughout the New Testament, has traditionally been translated as "fellowship," but he proposes that a better translation is "partnership."[59]

Not only is *partnership* a more inclusive and less sexist term, but it connotes more effectively the kind of Christian relationship envisioned in the New Testament, especially in Paul's letters. The difference is dramatic. For example, you might care for another "fellow" because it is the right thing to do. You do not wish another "fellow" harm. But if you have a business *partner* or a marriage *partner,* you care about what that person does, knowing that her or his life affects yours. Fellowship has come to mean a detached caring, while partnership is involving and engaging, recognizing the interdependence of all in the community. Partnership describes the kind of caring Paul wanted for the Christian community when he said, "If one member suffers, all suffer together; if one member is honored, all rejoice together" (1 Corinthians 12:26). Imagine how your expectations would differ if instead of walking into a fellowship hall, expecting coffee and a stale donut, you were entering a partnership hall.

A change in language can help us envision a different kind of church, a church that functions as a community, providing support and encouragement to its members. There are no easy steps to becoming a community, but each congregation could begin by assessing the needs of its own members and providing a vision of the future community. Mary Cosby, a partner in the Church of the Savior, Washington, D.C., suggests:

> One could begin by bringing together those people within the congregation desiring this deeper transforming intimacy. They could begin meeting together weekly in serious prayer and Bible study, in open, honest sharing and mutual accountability, and to seek to hear God's call through regular contact with the suffering poor.[60]

Of course, care must be taken to ensure that these groups serve to enhance the sense of community of the whole church and do not split the congregation. No venture of this sort will be risk-free, but with proper preparation, the needs of the whole congregation can be kept in mind. The benefits, on the other hand, are enormous:

> Our communal relationships serve as discipline, mutual correction, and help us in discerning God's will. The community of faith . . . becomes the critical community in our spiritual search. A vital role of the church in our day is the rebuilding of community.[61]

What will the congregation look like who attempts to meet the spiritual needs of its members *and* reach out to the world? There is not one blueprint to follow. Some churches may look more like the Sojourners community, engaged in direct service to the poor. Some may choose to concentrate on study and research; others may decide to give generously of their resources. All will find that the challenges of spiritual growth and social justice are interrelated. Throughout the centuries, the church has been most effective when it has boldly faced the challenges of its particular place and its particular era. The challenges of our place and era are great. The possibilities that await us when we meet our challenges are greater. The joy that is found in partnerships, in simpler living, and in community is the joy of the great banquet.

5

The Word and the Community

The Sunday after Christmas has been observed as "Student Sunday" at Central Church for years. Even though most of its students attend college near home and commute daily, the church still observes Student Sunday. The commuting students plan the service and reserve certain parts for those who go to school away from home.

Everyone knew that Pam would want a part in the service. Although she was a sophomore at an out-of-state college, she was in church all summer and kept in touch with calls and notes throughout the fall. In high school she was president of the youth group and an officer in the state youth organization. She was the best speaker of all the church's youth.

When the students rehearsed the service on Saturday, Pam read the prayer she had written. In a clear and unwavering voice she prayed:

> Parent of us all, you have brought us forth out of the womb of your being and named us your daughters and sons . . . in the spirit of the one who creates, redeems, and sustains us, the gracious and tender God. Amen.

During the coffee hour on Sunday several people asked the pastor what he thought of Pam's prayer. He was heard to say, "Well, it was different."

Guideline: *A congregation seeking to develop the spirituality of its members will help them understand the power of* *language and to become comfortable with lesser-known biblical images of God.*

The Power of the Word

"Sticks and stones may break my bones but words will never hurt me!" So goes an old school-ground chant. It argues that physical injury is more dangerous than psychological injury, that objects can hurt but "mere" words are harmless. The chant responds to verbal abuse as the victim tries to convince the attacker that even though the target was hit no damage was done.

That chant never convinced anyone — neither the attacker nor the victim! At their best, those words were a smoke screen sent up by the victim to slow the pace of the battle while the damage was assessed.

Everyone knows that words *can* hurt, do hurt, and that their damage is far more permanent than the damage caused by "sticks and stones." Muscles, nerves, fatty tissue, and even bones have their innate ability to heal. But if personalities can heal themselves, the healing time is much slower. It takes longer for a shattered spirit to get well than it does for a broken bone to mend.

Words have power. They have power to destroy. They have power to heal. And they have power to create. So words must be considered when spirituality is explored, learned, and practiced.

Let us recognize at the outset that spirituality is more than a verbal discipline. Proper speech does not ensure the desired relationship with the Divine. If we are only concerned with learning the right words, our spiritual growth will be stunted at the rational level and will not develop into full maturity. If the proper wording of a prayer, the correct name for the Divine, the best translation of the Bible, and the oldest version of a hymn were to become the goal of our spiritual quest, we should not be surprised if our spirituality remains undeveloped. Spirituality is more than a word game.

Let us also acknowledge that the absence of speech is as important a part of spiritual development as the selection of the right word. An oriental convert to the Christian faith once observed that Christianity was a very "talky" religion. Since silence cannot be talked about or analyzed without destroying its own genius, we simply state that spiritual development in its individual and corporate dimensions must allow silence its opportunity to heal, promote growth, and unite.

Few of us are ever silent. We are uncomfortable living in a quiet environment, preferring mindless chatter to silence. If we are not producing sound, we are consuming it. The television assaults us in our home, the radio accompanies us on our drive to work. Piped-in music or a desk radio provide background noise on the job. Headphones are strapped to our ears as we exercise. Cassette recorders are plugged in as we go across the campus. We wonder how much teenage violence can be attributed to this aural invasion, even if the lyrics themselves are not provocative. And, likewise, we wonder how much adult loneliness is made more acute because the noise of television, radio, and recordings make it impossible for creative silence to restore the individual's unity with the source of life. Whatever is said about the power of speech should not be understood as an attack on the power of silence.

Protestants, in particular, can learn from the mystics who valued and practiced silence to the exclusion of all speech. They have helped us understand that silence is its own confession to God, since everything that is said about God qualifies the Divine in some way. Thus, to say nothing about God, to admire God in silence, according to mystical logic, is to say everything about God!

The Name and the Community

The power of speech is affirmed early in the biblical story. The story of creation in the second chapter of Genesis pictures the human figure giving "names to all cattle, and to the birds of the air, and to every beast of the field" (Genesis 2:20). Thus the human shares with the Divine the ability to identify, sort, and signify all of the rest of the earth's creatures. The ability to assign names to objects separates the human from the less-than-human and elevates the human to near-divine standing.

The people of God did not become a distinctive group until God's name was revealed. When God appeared to Moses in a burning bush, Moses first learned who God was: "I am the God of Abraham, the God of Isaac, and the God of Jacob." But the story is incomplete until the name of the deity is revealed. Moses realized that his people would want to know the name of the god he had met.

> Then Moses said to God, "If I come to the people of Israel and say to them, 'The God of your fathers has sent me to you,' and they ask me, 'What is his name?' what shall I say to them?" God said to Moses, "I AM WHO I AM. . . . and thus I am to be remembered throughout all generations" (Exodus 3:13-15).

Popular theology remembers the encounter of Moses with the burning bush as a story of the miraculous presence of God. A more thoughtful reading of the story tells us that it is disclosure of the name of God that gives this story its lasting importance.

The disclosure of God's name to Moses shows that the biblical faith is rooted in relationship. When God appears in the Bible, loyalties are established, a community is formed, a nation is established. Those who meet this God find themselves engaged in fulfilling a mission. Sometimes the mission is to seek a land. Sometimes it is to purify worship. Sometimes it is to establish justice. When the biblical God is met, the result is the creation of a people with a mission.

There are other ways to think of God, other categories that can be put to use. Some philosophers speak of an "immanent" God. According to this view, the life of God is one with the life of the universe. Instead of being an absentee landlord who expects the tenants to fix up the house and pay the rent, this God is a resident manager whose purposes cannot be separated from the purposes of the property.

Other thinkers believe that God lives distinct and apart from the creation. They claim that God transcends this world and cannot be identified with the natural order. God can be appreciated in the beauty, orderliness, and power of nature, but God cannot be known in that fashion. Humans, if they are to know God, must depend on God and wait upon God until a revelation occurs.

Those are two familiar ways that philosophers discuss God. Even though these are primarily philosophical terms, they point to understandings of God that are commonly expressed in the typical Protestant church. A single service of worship may well include references to both the immanent and the transcendent God. The service might begin with the hymn "Immortal, Invisible, God Only Wise." That hymn, which stresses the transcendent grandeur of God, might be followed shortly by the congregation praying, "Our Father who art in heaven, hallowed be thy name." A worship leader might also direct a prayer to God described as "nearer than breathing, closer than hands or feet."

Although both distance and closeness may be part of worship, neither of these adequately fulfills the needs of the spirit. Religious speech cannot be limited to categories that describe either God's closeness or God's distance. The spiritual quest is a quest for relationship, so spatial language needs to be replaced by relational language.

Sallie McFague helps us see that relationships rather than space should form the basis for our religious speech:

> Unless one has a sense of the nearness of God, the overwhelming sense of the way God pervades and permeates our very being, one will not find religious images significant: the power of the images for God as father, mother, lover, friend, will not be appreciated.[62]

New Words and New Discoveries

Several thinkers are helping us see the inadequacy of much of our religious language, challenging us to question that speech, and to discover new and more valid terms and titles. As women have reflected on their experiences, they have found traditional language inadequate and have begun to find new terms that more adequately voice their own spiritual hungers and discoveries.

A leading theologian, Barbara Brown Zikmund, has retraced her own spiritual development and discovered four phases in it. Brown Zikmund first became troubled by the use of generic language in everyday speech:

> Words like "mankind," "brotherhood" and the overused pronoun "he" were supposed to describe all humanity. But it was clear that they contained a masculine bias. Little girls were hearing those words literally and scaling down their self-image.

Brown Zikmund decided that even if she was not personally troubled by such talk, she should react to it as a matter of justice. "Language both reflects the way we think and informs what we think."

At the second stage, she began to be bothered by the masculine bias in reference to God. "If Christians insist that God is without gender, why do we call God 'he' at every turn?" This was an important but troubling stage, for although she rejected "gender-specific" language, she continued to believe God was personal. The question, "How could God be personal and not male or female?" pursued her at this stage.

At the third stage Brown Zikmund began to use both male and female terms for God. Her prayers focused on God's feminine qualities in an effort to seek balance.

At the fourth stage Brown "reclaimed a very old and very important Christian way of speaking about God: the doctrine of the Trinity." She acknowledges that on one level "the trinitarian formula of God as Father, Son, and Holy Spirit is totally unacceptable — an old man, a young man, and a dove." But Brown Zikmund did not return to the Trinity because of its terminology. She reclaimed the Trinity because the doctrine expressed what she was beginning to discover in her own experience — that reality is relational and communal:

> To believe in a triune God is to suggest that there is an inner relational energy within Godself which spills over into the Christian life. . . . When we worship a triune God we celebrate the love which flows in God's eternal dance of togetherness, and which we know through Jesus Christ as Lord of the dance.[63]

Now we begin to see that the matter of language cannot be resolved just by deciding to use inclusive language when referring to humans or descriptions and titles of God that avoid the matter of gender. What is involved is a new way of thinking, a new consciousness. At stake now is not words, important as they are, but a vision of reality. As John Cobb puts it:

> to change one's habits of speech, many of us can testify, is also a consciousness-raising event. It forces us to examine the images associated with the words and the habits of mind and attitudes associated with these images.[64]

From Oppression — Insight

In the 1830s and 1840s women began to assume new roles in North American society. As they studied the Bible, their study was enriched by their new experiences. One result was the publication of *The Woman's Bible*, a collaborative effort of some twenty women, completed in the 1880s. This was an early effort to respond to the masculine bias women recognized in the Bible. The publication of *An Inclusive Language Lectionary*, a current effort, is giving people of today an opportunity to hear and study the Bible in language that is appropriate for a God who shows "inclusive love for all people."[65] The lectionary declares that its mandate is to seek

> language which expresses inclusiveness with regard to human beings and which attempts to expand the range of images beyond the masculine to assist the church in understanding the full nature of God.[66]

In the century between *The Woman's Bible* and *An Inclusive Language Lectionary*, significant developments were taking place among women inside and outside of the church. Women in different countries and cultures began to discover each other, drawn together by their awareness of common conditions of oppression, though expressed in different ways.

As Christian women continued to study their biblical heritage, they did not discover a warrant for the physical, political, and psychological oppression they were experiencing. Rather, they learned that the biblical revelation had been interpreted and translated by men whose own views affected the way the revelation was recorded. As women continued their study, new insights broke upon them:

> Throughout the centuries, interpreters of scripture have explored the male language of faith, full and overflowing. Yet the Bible itself proclaims another dimension that faith has lost--female imagery and motifs.[67]

A century-and-a-half of struggle and discovery is providing new opportunities for spiritual discovery today. The opportunities are available to all, both male and female:

> This entire searching, rediscovering, casting away and selecting process in which women are engaged, is a means of finding a new humanity not only for themselves but for humankind as a whole. For we might in these days witness a spiritual revolution pointing to a new humanity which is possible only because Christ lived and taught us radically new possibilities and gave us a radically new image of God and humanity.[68]

It is precisely the image of God that is so threatening — and promising — for people seeking to deepen their spiritual life today. Biblical scholars, male and female, have discovered that *father* as used in the Bible has a different meaning from *father* as used in our time. They have also discovered other biblical images of God that cannot be associated with the male gender.

In biblical times *father* was not a term that referred to a single, authoritarian, male individual. The term suggested a corporate life, which it does not signify today. *Father* was *pater familias*, the father of the household, something unfamiliar today:

> The authority of the father within the household was absolute, extending through wife, children, and servants, who, in a sense, were regarded as extensions of the father. Servants could speak and act for the *pater familias* in the same way as Moses is able to speak in the person of God.[69]

Today *father* is not a term that stands for a group of related people of many ages and both genders. Today the term points to a single individual, often absent from the family, who nevertheless exerts control over that group.

> Thus, while the use of the term Father may have had the sense of the corporate personality of God within the biblical world, the translator must also take account of the use of the term Father within the contemporary world on a number of levels. Not only has the term "Father" lost the connotation of the representative of the household or kin group and the care and support shared in the group, but it has *regained* a sense of one-sided power over other members of the family which was, in fact, challenged by Jesus' relationship with God as *Abba*.[70]

The frequent use of *Father* should not distract us from many other terms used in the Bible. Today's scholars call attention to several instances where feminine imagery is used to describe God. The significance of these references mounts when we remember that they originated in a male-oriented environment. The following references are frequently cited:

Isaiah 66:13	God as a mother who comforts
Psalm 131:2	God as a mother who quieted a child at her breast.
Isaiah 46:3	People of Israel carried in the womb of God.

Deuteronomy 32:18	God as mother of Israel
Psalm 17:8	God as mother bird
Psalm 36:7	God as mother bird
Psalm 57:1	God as mother bird
Psalm 91:4	God as mother bird.[71]

The experience of women, as understood and interpreted in the twentieth century, will give new dimensions to spirituality in today's congregation. What will be noticed will be the different language. But that language will be an expression of reality that has deeply affected millions of women, and men too, in our day. This new language points to a new vision of authority that is more communal than imperial, more participatory than dictatorial, more cooperative than autocratic. The experience of women challenges a system where things are "assigned a divine order, with God at the top, men next, and so down to dogs, plants, and 'impersonal' nature."[72]

Congregational Consequences

Some congregations are exploring the use of inclusive language and considering what that use might mean. These churches are unwilling to leave the matter in the hands of theologians, worship specialists, and denominational program leaders. They want to provide for their members opportunities for spiritual discovery that a new vocabulary can offer.

If worship were not important, it would not matter what is said, sung, played, displayed, or worn. But worship exposes people to reality and provides the way for people to become connected to that reality. Thus the words and actions of worship make deep marks on the human spirit. The importance of worship argues for careful planning of worship experiences and the exercise of caution when changes in established patterns of speech or action are being made. Changes in the way we speak of God, or the way we behave in worship, can be deeply troubling, because changes call into question our own spiritual life.

The power of worship to shape identity is found in the encounter between the divine and the human during the sacred assembly. That designated time and place enables a new dynamic to take place between God and the gathered people of God. At the very heart of the occasion is the reading and hearing of the divine revelation, the very focus of which is the power of God to forge human identity and to shape human history anew.[73]

A radical change in worship practice can be as disturbing as the discovery that the hospital where one was born is now being used as a warehouse for old computers.

Some congregations see no reason for examining their worship vocabulary, for there are no people in the church who are raising the issue. The people who might be offended by male-dominated language, lessons, and hymns have never attended that church, have quietly withdrawn to a more hospitable place — or to no place at all. For these churches the issue is too distant and academic to be taken seriously.

Many congregations resist changes in the language of lessons, prayers, and sermons because they continue to be dominated by men who find the feminine preferences either difficult to appreciate or deeply threatening. Even though the number of women in both pulpit and elected positions in North American churches is increasing, men still remain in control of most churches, and most men have yet to appropriate and value the distinctive experiences that women are bringing to the church.

Church leaders, both lay and clergy, tend to see proposed changes in church vocabulary as political strategy. Their resistance to change stiffens if they perceive the change as a feminist tactic to call attention to the way women have been treated in the church. Protectors of the status quo need to be convinced that the language issue is a spiritual matter, not a political one.

Many of the people most resistant to change proposed by women are other women. These resisters realize that the change in religious language calls into question their own self-image and their own spiritual formation. Some middle-aged and older women, whose prayers and work have kept thousands of churches alive before present feminists were born, perceive new worship language as a direct attack upon them. Inclusive language often finds its toughest opponents among the faithful and older worshipers in countless churches, large and small.

In the twentieth century, people have changed, and they have learned how to change. This period has taught us that people do not think themselves into changing. They act themselves into changing. Although racial segregation still mars the national character, it was dealt a mortal blow by the Supreme Court decision that banned "separate but equal" public school facilities. When the Supreme Court ordered change, people pleaded for more time. They wanted to delay change in behavior until white people had had an opportunity to change their attitudes toward black people. Now, over twenty-five years later, it is clear that attitudes have changed because behavior changed. We realize now that without the court order requiring integration we would still be talking about equality — while sitting in segregated facilities.

As congregations try out new language, they will gain appreciation for the pioneers who first spoke it — and the bondage from which they came. Those speaking the new language of inclusion will recognize how the old language excluded people — and the effects of that inclusion.

> Those who say that this concern of women for language that is whole, positive, and inclusive is unreasonable should begin to think about what it is like to sit through years of lectures, sermons, instructions, etc., in which one is never named, even by inclusion in the pronouns used.[74]

Praying, Singing, Reading

As congregations try out new language, they will enter the new world they are voicing. The language of that new world will liberate them from a world more confining than they had realized. The result will be an awakened spirituality enlivened by an image of God inclusive of both male and female and extended by a host of other biblical images that have been obscured by male-oriented language and ways of thinking. What must now be discussed are ways that new language can be uttered in the typical church. The issue of speech leads to some practical questions:

Is it still "Okay" to say, "In the name of the Father, Son, and the Holy Spirit," or are there new words to use?
What about "Our Father who art in heaven"?
Shall we decide never to sing "Rise Up, O Men of God"?
What about "Onward Christian Soldiers"?

An individual has complete freedom when praying alone. She or he can address God in whatever language seems meaningful and employ whatever images are helpful. But we have set spirituality in a congregational context. That means that language, written and verbal, spoken and sung, must be considered carefully.

> Worship . . . is not merely our natural human response to the reality of God within our lives, but more importantly a vital setting wherein God is encountered. How this reality is articulated, the language used to describe and foster it, is a powerful shaper of our own identity and of our conceptualization of God.[75]

If we are to speak publicly of God, what choices lie before us? What are the symbols available to us as we speak of the Divine?

Speaking of the Trinity

If a helpful and honest way of referring to the Trinity can be developed, the language issue is well on its way toward resolution. The Trinity is central to the Christian understanding of God. Yet its traditional formulation, "Father, Son, and Holy Spirit," seems to present the problem of male-dominated language without offering any clues regarding its solution.

Rebecca Oxford-Carpenter has discovered seven ways the "gender Trinity issue" can be treated. The result is a virtual catalog of available ways for the Christian to speak of God.

Two centuries after Jesus, the early church began to speak of God in three *personae*. The word *persona* originally was a mask worn by an actor in a play. At the time this formula was developed, the social and political role of women was being neutralized and masculine images of God were being stressed. The first two terms are obviously masculine. But the Spirit, the third *persona* of the Trinity, was also considered to be masculine, even though the word for *spirit* in Hebrew is a feminine word and the word for *spirit* in Greek is a neuter word. This formulation represents the non-feminine way of speaking of the Trinity and seems to deny any feminine attributes of God.

Although not strictly trinitarian, Goddess religion often appears as a reaction to theological language that ignores the feminine altogether. "The renewed interest in Goddess religion is an understandable and even refreshing reaction to worship of the all-masculine divine images of the Christian church, much as the Black Power movement was an expectable backlash against white supremacy." Oxford-Carpenter believes that such a religion could result in "reverse sexism" and could lead to the oppression of women because of its reliance on stereotypes.

A third way to speak of the Trinity is to find within each *persona* both masculine and feminine traits. This approach assumes that God's fullness cannot be captured by images of one gender. According to this view, God is not just Father, King, and Lord; God is also our Mother, Queen, and Lady.

The psychologist Carl Jung once proposed that the Trinity be expanded into a "quaternity," legitimizing the feminine within the Divine. This would satisfy the needs Jung discovered in his own work for a feminine expression of God. This fourth *persona* of the Trinity would satisfy the needs of the unconscious mind for the feminine expression.

A fifth way of expression of the Trinity is one developed by theologians and biblical scholars who used non-sexual images of the three *personae* of the Trinity. Some desexed images include Friend, Comforter, Redeemer, Savior, Liberator, Love Teacher, Sustainer, Comrade, Creator, Messiah, Maker, and Advocate. Augustine developed his own substitutes for the traditional formula. Three of his substitutes were: (1) Lover, Loved, Love (2) Speaker, Hearer, and Sense in Between, and (3) Seer, Seen, and Light in Between.

The sixth method is to speak of God in a depersonalized as well as a desexed way. Some of the examples, and those who have developed them, are:

God in the World, God in Christ, and God in the church (Schleiermacher).

God in creation, God in history, God in present tense (Trueblood).

God everywhere and always, God there and then, and God here and now (Read).

Memory, Understanding, and Will (Augustine).

Love Originating, Love Responding, and Love Uniting (Aquinas).

Book-as-Thought, Book-as-Written, and Book-as-Read (Sayers).

In commenting on all six treatments of the Trinity, Oxford-Carpenter finds the first three "flawed from the start." The first two suppress the masculine or the feminine. The solution of Jung is also unbalanced.

She thinks the other three offer promise and have biblical precedent. Her solution draws upon the strengths discovered. She suggests "multiple metaphors for God: masculine, feminine, non-sexual, and depersonalized." In using "multiple metaphors," she insists that there be relationship between the *personae* and that the worshipers also have relation to each *persona*. The result, according to Oxford-Carpenter, is the opportunity to "begin to reflect a God of multiple aspect, a magnificent, shocking, wonderful, loving God . . . . As we let God be seen as whole, we ourselves become whole, and one of the major aims of religion is fulfilled." [76]

This summary of ways of speaking of the Trinity shows that we are not locked into the "Father, Son, and Holy Spirit" formula. Although the Bible and church tradition offer basic understandings of God, the ancient expressions should not prevent today's worshiper from saying what God means in this era. Whatever we say about God, even our most carefully crafted language will never adequately express the divine nature.

"Shall We Stand and Sing?"

People enjoying the freedom of new language and reflecting on the reality behind that language may find their enthusiasm quickly smothered when they open the hymnal. Many hymns are not only captive to the male-domination of another era but also to the cultural and national impulses of the late nineteenth and early twentieth century that often confused church establishment with market development and overseas missionary work with national promotion.

It takes years to produce a hymnal, yet words change in a matter of months. So it is a "given" that hymnals will be out-of-date by the time they are first available to the local congregation.

There are no simple ways to solve the problem of the outdated and often offensive language of hymns. Sometimes a word or a phrase can be changed and that change simply announced when the hymn is to be sung. At other times it may be necessary to provide a revision of the hymn's words and announce the tune to be used. Of course, copyright laws must be honored!

There are some hymns whose message is not limited by the outdated language. We sing them and recognize with humility that some day people will look at the views of our own age with wonder and exasperation. Few of us want to throw out "A Mighty Fortress Is Our God" even though we would argue with Luther about "this world with devils filled."

Of course, there are some hymns whose male imagery is so pervasive or whose military language so offensive that those hymns must be ignored. It is usually better to ignore such a hymn completely than attempt to make it acceptable by clumsy revisions, inept substitutions, or awkward announcements. Uncomfortable worshipers are not apt to be converted to inclusive language. They just want to sit down and move on to the next part of the service!

The discovery of inclusive language can be an educational experience for the congregation, broadening the awareness of all. And for some it will be an act of liberation. Racist, sexist, and militaristic language has caused some worshipers to remain mute during most services. But inclusive language will allow them to make a joyful noise once again.

"Here Begins the Lesson"

Since 1983 there have been suggested readings from the Old Testament and the New Testament for each Sunday of the year in a common lectionary acceptable to Anglicans, Roman Catholics, and most Protestants. This widespread attention to the same lessons by worshiping Christians is binding believers together and preparing them for more visible forms of Christian unity.

In 1986 *An Inclusive Language Lectionary* was published through the leadership of the National Council of Churches. A committee of biblical scholars and church leaders recast the readings of the new lectionary into inclusive language. This effort was "to provide both to reader and to hearer a sense of belonging to a Christian faith community in which truly all are one in Christ." [77]

While keeping in mind the desire of both men and women to hear the word of God without cultural biases, the *Inclusive Language Lectionary* also addresses people of color who are troubled by phrases that associate darkness with evil and light with good. Attention has also been paid to those with physical impairments so that their conditions would not be interpreted judgmentally in the act of reading and hearing the Bible. Finally, the lectionary seeks to reduce tensions between Jews and Christians by giving attention to texts that have cast "the Jews" as enemies of Christ when that term referred to the religious leadership of the day rather than to Jews as they are now identified. Thus, efforts have been made to remove obstacles that human culture has erected that tend to keep women, the people of color, and the physically impaired from hearing the Bible unconditionally. They also seek to remove unnecessary barriers between Christians and Jews.

A congregation might employ *An Inclusive Language Lectionary* in at least three ways. The Sunday readings from the lectionary could be printed as each worshiper may read along as the lessons are read aloud. Or the congregation may read from pew Bibles as the lessons are read from the new translation. This experience would help the people understand the new insights provided by inclusive language. Or, of course, the lessons may simply be read from the *Inclusive Language Lectionary*, with the leader citing not only the references but the source as well.

Occasionally the congregation should be invited to read the lessons in unison using inclusive language. The sound of different words and phrases are less threatening when heard in one's own voice.

Congregations concerned about spiritual maturity will welcome the sound of inclusive language because that language invites people who have felt alienation and separation. Inclusive language is by implication, if not by definition, a language of evangelism. There are women, and men too, who yearn for fellowship with those who see God affirming oneness rather than tribalism, inclusion rather than exclusion. Inclusive language encourages people who look for wholeness to lay down the burdens of competition and separateness and rejoice in the unity of all people in Jesus Christ.

Speaking of God, reading the Bible, praying, and singing are basic activities of any Christian body. Because of the power words possess, the spiritually aware congregation chooses them carefully. The language it uses witnesses to God whose unity and universal love is promised to all. This community is strengthened as the Scriptures are read and the good news proclaimed in a systematic way. Yet this community is not lodged in the past; it stands in the present, leaning toward the future.

We are all looking for a church where spirituality is not a project but an assumption. In this church the members share in the worship, mission, and maintenance activities with full commitment. Their church work does not drain energy from them but makes them stronger. In this church, committee work is as satisfying as a prayer retreat. The members of this church view spirituality as "a way of being in the world," so they work and witness for justice and attend to local needs. The people in this congregation have modest expectations because they know their limitations. Yet they find genuine joy in serving because work and witness have become united in a common expression of faith.

In this church of our common quest people do not attempt to organize spirituality nor lobby for it. Instead, spirituality forms the fabric of their common life.

6

Ideas and Events

There is an acute hunger for spirituality in churches every-where. Church leaders and ordinary pew-sitters, lay people and clergy, recognize it and feel it themselves. As the hunger for deeper spirituality grows, so grow the opportunities to meet the need. Books, records, tapes, videocassettes, retreats, and workshops of all sorts are available. Church leaders now have the opportunity to select the menu, to recommend a diet to meet the spiritual hunger. The cafeteria of spiritual choices offers solitary retreats, medita-tion techniques, prayer groups, and exercises, to name just a few.

The preceding chapters have laid a foundation for decision-making. They have tested today's spiritual climate, suggested what the individual should expect in spiritual growth, stressed the integration of spirituality and social justice, and pointed out the role of language in spiritual development. Through it all has been the persistent belief that "the congregation is the place."

Here are some suggested guidelines for spiritual growth in the congregation:

The programs should invite every member to experience a new dimension of church and guard against spiritual elitism.

The programs should be adaptable to congregations of all sizes.

The programs should take place in church facilities or mem-bers' homes whenever possible.

The programs should reinforce the worship life of the congre-gation.

What follows are specific proposals that meet those guidelines. These suggestions may lead people to observe, "We can do that." It would be even better if these suggestions were to prompt people to say, "That gives me an idea!"

Using the Church Year as a Planning Guide

PURPOSE   To allow the congregation's worship to provide the framework for planning and program. To allow the spiritual significance of the seasons of the church year to impact the life of the congregation.

DESCRIPTION   This scheme takes the six seasons of the church's worship life, gives each season a planning focus and theme, and develops programs and events around the themes. (Although September and October actually mark the final weeks of the Pentecost season, this scheme begins in September since that is the normal start-up time for most churches.)

Season	Theme	Events
Pentecost (final weeks)	"Season of Learning for Doing"	Bible lectureship in September to launch the program year. Stewardship education.
Advent-Christmas	"The Season of Giving and Receiving"	Financial campaign for next calendar year. Christmas offering.
Epiphany	"The Season of Concern"	Study of local social needs. Engagement in local mission. "One Great Hour of Sharing." Examination of public policy toward the poor.

Lent	"Discovering and Following Christ's Way"	Church membership classes. Prayer breakfasts. Home Bible Study. Visitation for church membership. Palm Sunday. Maundy Thursday observance. Easter Eve baptisms.
Easter	"Being God's People"	Planning for summer and fall. Membership cultivation. Building maintenance. Beautification of grounds.
Pentecost (June—August)	"Growing in God's Favor"	Vacation Church School. Youth camp. Leadership recruitment. Denominational celebrations.

REQUIREMENTS   A planning event where each committee surveys the seasons of the church year and their planning themes.

A Planning Council[78]

PURPOSE

To integrate necessary church tasks and programs into the spiritual life of the congregation.

DESCRIPTION

In this model there is a planning team of approximately five persons for each of the seasons of the church year: Advent, Christmas, Epiphany, Lent, Pentecost. All of the planning teams comprise the Planning Council, which envisions the congregation's life for a full year. Each planning team develops the programs and events appropriate to its season and then calls on the various committees in the church to assist in carrying out the programs and events.[79] For example:

Advent Planning Team

Projects and Events	Leadership
Caroling to Homebound	Membership Committee arranges for homes, provides gifts, organizes transportation, publicizes event.

Christmas Offering	Outreach Committee sets goals, orders materials, publicizes event:
	    speakers
	    letters
	    posters
	    church newsletters

Advent Meditation Booklet	Worship Department enlists writers, prepares copy, arranges printing, mails booklets.
Etc.	Etc.

REQUIREMENTS Recruitment of necessary number of people with skills in planning. Council must have its calendar completed at least three months before first event is to occur.

Home Bible Study in Lent

PURPOSE
To deepen spirituality through small group Bible study.
To develop the home as a site for spiritual growth.
To develop the leadership of lay people.

DESCRIPTION
During each week in Lent, Bible study takes place in homes throughout the congregation, with ten to twelve people in each group. The church staff selects the themes and develops study activities to be used in each session. This material is recorded on audiotape. In each study site a lay leader conducts the meeting and carries out the activities called for on the tape. Leaders may be deacons, elders, church school teachers, or other officers. Themes can be biblical topics that can be studied in a six-week period, such as "Table Talk with Jesus," "Our Favorite Parables of Jesus," or "The Crowd at Calvary." Each session includes study, group participation, and prayer.

REQUIREMENTS
Host homes for six weeks.
Group leaders for each session.
Production and duplication of study tapes.

Maundy Thursday at Home

PURPOSE
To experience the intimacy that characterized the Last Supper.
To enhance the peoples' experience of Holy Week.
To deepen the congregation's fellowship life.

DESCRIPTION
For the observance of Holy Communion on Maundy Thursday, the congregation is invited to receive communion in the homes of church members. (This service could be a continuation of "Home Bible Study in Lent.") The service can follow the denominational liturgy, or portions could be prepared by the church staff and recorded on audiotape. Bread for the service can be baked by children or young people on Palm Sunday, blessed in church that day, and then taken to the homes where Maundy Thursday is to be observed.

REQUIREMENTS
Homes to host the event.
Elements properly prepared for holy communion.
A liturgy for holy communion, with required leaders.

World Communion Sunday

PURPOSE   To deepen participation in the worldwide Christian community.

DESCRIPTION   This observance of World Communion Sunday uses cultural and national differences to highlight the unity that exists within the body of Jesus Christ. In the worship service people with non-English background read the lessons in the language of their homeland. Instead of usual communion bread, the bread for this service represents the backgrounds of the people of the congregation: German bread, pita bread, French bread, tortillas, etc. When possible, the bread is baked in the homes of church members. Bread not consumed during communion is enjoyed with coffee, tea, and punch by the worshipers following the service. Vocal music in language other than English further strengthens the experience.

REQUIREMENTS   Readers for non-English scripture lessons. Bread from other lands bought by or prepared by church members from those countries. Music with non-English words.

A Tour of Church Facilities

PURPOSE

To ensure that church buildings, equipment, and furnishings are supporting the spiritual growth of the congregation.

To discover needed repairs and redecoration.

To develop an awareness of the influence of the physical environment on spiritual growth.

DESCRIPTION

This annual tour of all church facilities, including classrooms, offices, storerooms, restrooms, recreation areas, and rehearsal space involves key staff people, church leadership, and those responsible for building maintenance. One person serves as leader of the tour and maintains two checklists, one for rooms and physical facilities, and one for equipment and furnishings. The tour leader asks all participants these questions and records their answers. Checklist for Rooms and Other Space:

1. Who uses this room and for what purpose?
2. Is this space being used to its full potential?
3. How could this space be better used?
4. When was this room last painted?
5. Imagine walking into the room for the first time. What statement does it make?
6. Does this space encourage a simple and honest approach to the gospel, or are there furnishings and decoration that detract from an ordered life? Checklist for Equipment and Furniture:
1. When was this equipment last used?
2. What meanings surround this item?
3. Is this item in good repair?
4. Should we make plans to replace this item?

REQUIREMENTS

Clipboard

Pencil

Checklists

Old clothes to wear

A Sermon Seminar

PURPOSE

To develop the congregation's awareness of and appreciation for disciplined Bible study.
To prepare sermons that represent the congregation's questions and affirmations.

DESCRIPTION

In this seminar the people join the pastor in Bible study and discussion of lectionary selections in preparation for the sermon. In each weekly session the lectionary lessons for a Sunday two weeks in the future are read, studied, and discussed. Commentaries and other resources are used. In each session one person is responsible for each of the lessons, doing research about the reading, and suggesting ways the sermon might develop. Class members are expected to read all selections and share their insights with the group. This method of Bible study is especially well-suited for a limited period of time such as Lent. The class will also want to discuss the most recent sermon preached, noting how their study and discussion influenced the sermon.

REQUIREMENTS

Bibles
Commentaries
Concordances
Bible atlas

An Outreach Fair

PURPOSE
To develop awareness and support for world mission and local outreach efforts.

To make Epiphany a meaningful time for a congregation.

DESCRIPTION
This is a Sunday event replacing church school classes with booths, displays, and demonstrations of mission and outreach work that require the support of churches. Taking place during Epiphany, it shows how the light of the gospel is being projected in today's world. The event can take place in any large area such as a dining room, fellowship hall, or gym. Local agencies such as food banks, shelters, youth organizations, and senior citizen advocacy groups are invited to set up displays and provide interpreters and literature. Denominational and ecumenical outreach work can be represented by members of the congregation's outreach committee who are prepared to distribute literature and answer questions. Balloons, popcorn, clowns, and circus music add to the carnival atmosphere.

REQUIREMENTS
Contact local agencies.

Gather material from denominational and ecumenical outreach offices.

Arrange for carnival atmosphere with appropriate decorations, refreshments, entertainment. Publicize the event in local press, church newsletters and posters.

Spiritual Retreat for Youth

PURPOSE
: To introduce high-school-age youth to the benefits of the spiritual life.

  To show youth that the spiritual life is a part of their *whole* life.

DESCRIPTION
: The retreat is co-led by an adult familiar to and well-liked by the group, and an adult with expertise in the area of relating spirituality to youth. The retreat begins Friday at 6:00 p.m. and concludes Sunday at 8:00 a.m. The focus is that spiritual disciplines can enrich the whole of one's life: relationships, academics, athletics. The format includes the following elements:

  —Description of spiritual disciplines.

  —Discussion of what a "spiritually mature" person is like, followed by role plays showing how a spiritually mature person would cope with typical teenage situations.

  —Group-building exercises.

  —Small groups are responsible for preparation and cleanup of meals.

  —Divide into small groups for discussion and exercises related to topic.

  —Recreation time offers options of noncompetitive games, creative outlets with music and art.

  —Group has closing service at breakfast, then returns to home church for worship.

REQUIREMENTS
: Adult leaders, one for each group of four or five youth. Adequate facility.

  Food.

  Kids bring: pen, paper, Bibles, musical instruments, paints, easels, clay, etc.

Spiritual Retreat for Adults

PURPOSE

To provide individuals with an intense period of time in which they can experiment with spiritual disciplines.

To benefit from the experiences of someone familiar with spiritual disciplines.

To give individuals an experience they will want to repeat in their daily lives and share with others.

DESCRIPTION

Adults are invited to a weekend retreat, beginning Friday at 6:00 p.m., ending Sunday at noon. The location should be conducive to periods of quiet. The ideal location is a beautiful, natural setting. The retreat leader could be an outsider or a church member, someone familiar with the disciplines of the spiritual life. The format would include the following elements:

—Lectures about spiritual disciplines, such as prayer, meditation, Bible study.

—Group sharing.

—Individuals are invited to participate in each discipline. Time is set aside for silent prayer, guided prayer, meditation to music. Instructions on how to keep a prayer journal are given. Bible studies are held.

—Films about men and women who have led spiritually disciplined lives could be shown. Examples: Gandhi, Dorothy Day.

—Worship on Sunday morning, developed by group.

—Time for walks, conversations are provided.

—Meals are adequate, yet simple.

—Recreation time includes listening to music, sharing books, etc.

REQUIREMENTS

Capable leader.

Adequate facility.

Food.

Films and projector (or video equipment).

Taped music.

Communion for worship service.

Adults bring: paper and pens, Bibles.

Lenten Learning Celebration[80]

PURPOSE
To familiarize congregation with symbols of Lent. To encourage spiritual growth in Lent. To provide an opportunity for intergenerational togetherness.

DESCRIPTION
A pancake and sausage supper is held on Shrove Tuesday, the night before Ash Wednesday. The room is decorated with purple balloons or streamers, and purple napkins on the tables. After dinner, the projects can begin using one of two methods, depending on the size of the group and the size of the room. Either learning centers can be set up in advance and groups can move from project to project, or materials can be brought to each table so that each table works together until each project is completed.

Project #1: A poster is displayed, showing different Lenten symbols and different crosses. Each person is given pipe cleaners and told to make a Lenten symbol or a cross out of pipe cleaners.

Project #2: A brief explanation of the traditions of Lent is given. Each group is given old worship bulletins, religious magazines, glue, scissors, markers, and a large posterboard. Each group is to make a poster about the meaning of Lent.

Project #3: A brief explanation of spiritual disciplines is given. Each person is handed an index card on which to write a Lenten resolution.

When all have completed their projects, the posters are hung at one end of the room where a worship table has been set up. All gather at the worship center, seated. The Lenten resolutions are placed on the offering plate on the worship table. The worship table could be set with purple candles. Pretzels and grape juice are passed out. A brief meditation is given, one song is sung, and all partake of the pretzels and grape juice. The group is asked to stand, join hands, and pray together the Lord's Prayer. At the end of the prayer, the evening has ended.

REQUIREMENTS Group to prepare and serve pancake supper. (After dinner, they are invited to join an activity group.) Display posters. Pipe cleaners. Scissors. Old bulletins. Magazines. Glue. Markers. Posterboard. Pens. Index cards. Worship table with purple candles. Purple napkins. Purple streamers. Purple balloons. Offering basket. Pretzels. Grape juice. Leader.

Rite of Passage Upon
Receiving the Driver's License
"Celebration of Maturity"

PURPOSE

To have the congregation mark an important event in the lives of young people.

To impart on young people the responsibility a driver's license means.

DESCRIPTION

One or two times during the year depending upon the size of the congregation), all the young people who have recently received their driver's licenses are invited to participate in this ritual. It should take place at the point in the worship service where other such rituals are celebrated: baptisms, baby dedications, etc. The pastor calls the young people forward and says, "In the Bible we read that one of the marks of the Christian is maturity. Today we celebrate the growth taking place in your lives, not because of your age but because of your sense of responsibility. As young adults who have received your driver's licenses, will you please repeat after me the Covenant of Responsibility?"

Covenant: "As a licensed driver, I am aware of my responsibility to myself and to other people. Aware of our world's limited resources, I promise to consider carefully the purpose of each trip I take. As a child of God, my life is precious. I will not waste my time on useless driving, and I will not waste my body by abusing drugs or alcohol. These are my promises, made with my friends and my church family."

Congregational Response: "We affirm each of you as you have stepped into adulthood. We are proud of your growth and feel your joy on this day. We pledge that we will support you should you make mistakes, and will be here for you should you have questions."

At the end of the ritual, the pastor could have a prayer. Then each young person is given a symbol by which to remember the covenant. A keychain or bumpersticker would be appropriate. A special reception after church would further honor the young people.

REQUIREMENTS Pastor should meet with young people several weeks in advance of the ritual, to explain it to them and to invite them to have family and friends present. Litany printed in worship bulletin. Keychain or bumpersticker.

Notes

1. Tilden Edwards, *Living Simply Through the Day: Spiritual Survival in a Complex Age*. Paulist Press, 1977, p. 52.

2. Anthony C. Meisel and M.L. delMastro, *The Rule of St. Benedict*. Doubleday, 1975, p. 31.

3. Suzanne Gordon, *Lonely in America*. Simon and Schuster, 1976, p. 41.

4. Carol Ochs, *Women and Spirituality*. Rowman and Allanheld, 1983, p. 12.

5. Martin E. Marty, *Pilgrims in Their Own Land: 500 Years of Religion in America*. Little, Brown and Company, 1984, p. 227.

6. *Ibid*, p. 155–156.

7. *Ibid*, p. 156.

8. Robert N. Bellah, *Broken Covenant*. Seabury Press, 1977.

9. Tilden Edwards, *Ibid.*, p. 222.

10. Donald J. Wilcox, *In Search of God and Self: Renaissance and Reformation Thought*. Houghton Mifflin, 1975, p. 251.

11. Arthur Cushman McGiffert, *A History of Christian Thought*, Volume Two. Charles Scribner's Sons, 1953, p. 360.

12. Wilcox, *Ibid.*, p. 321.

13. Thomas Merton, *Contemplative Prayer*. Herder and Herder, 1969, pp. 94–95.

14. Robert N. Bellah, et al., *Habits of the Heart: Individualism and Commitment in American Life*. University of California Press, 1985, p. 233.

15. *Ibid.*, p. 221.

16. Marvin Kessler, S.J., and Bernard Brown, S.J., *Dimensions of the Future: The Spirituality of Teilhard de Chardin*. Corpus Books, 1968, p. 9.

17. *Ibid.*, p. 12.

18. Margaret R. Miles, *Fullness of Life: Historical Foundations for a New Asceticism*. Westminster, 1981, p. 158.

19. *Ibid.*

20. *Ibid.*, pp. 159ff.

21. Dieter T. Hessel, ed., *Social Themes of the Christian Year*. Geneva Press, 1983.

22. McGiffert, *Ibid.*, p. 370.

23. Mary McDermott Shideler, *In Search of the Spirit*. Ballantine Books, 1985, pp. 211–212.

24. *Ibid.*, p. 212.

25. Louisville *Courier-Journal*, October 19, 1987.

26. William Stringfellow, *The Politics of Spirituality*. Westminster, 1984, p. 32.

27. Urban T. Holmes, III, *A History of Christian Spirituality: An Analytical Introduction*. Seabury Press, 1980, p. 27.

28. *Ibid.*, p. 29–30.

29. Williston Walker, *A History of the Christian Church*. Charles Scribner's Sons, 1959, p. 95.

30. The World Council of Churches, *Baptism, Eucharist and Ministry*, 1982, p. 16.

31. Michael Kinnamon and Robert Welsh, *Baptism, Eucharist and Ministry: A Guide for Study*. Council on Christian Unity, 1984, p. 14.

32. The World Council of Churches, *Ibid.*, p. 23.

33. *Ibid.*

34. Gwen Kennedy Neville and John H. Westerhoff, III, *Learning Through Liturgy*. Seabury, 1978, p. 162.

35. Peter Monkres, "Doing Church Business in a Spiritual Manner," *The Christian Ministry*, November 1986, p. 14–16.

36. *Ibid.*, p. 15.

37. *Ibid.*, p. 15.

38. Donald L. Jones, "Faithful to God's Claim in Congregational Life," an address to the General Assembly of the Christian Church (Disciples of Christ), Louisville, Kentucky, October 19, 1987.

39. Eugene C. Roehlkepartain, "Unknown Waters," *The Christian Ministry*, November 1986, p. 2.

40. Mary Cosby, "Called to Intimacy, Called to Mission," *Christian Ministry*, November 1986, p. 12.

41. Stringfellow, *Ibid.*, p. 17.

42. *Ibid.*, p. 17–18.

43. Tom Frary, "Thy Kingdom Come," *America*, November 11, 1972, p. 385.

44. Matthew Fox, *A Spirituality Named Compassion*. Winston Press, 1979, p. iii.

45. John H. Westerhoff, III, *Inner Growth/Outer Change: An Educational Guide to Church Renewal*. Seabury Press, 1979, pp. 6–7.

46. Meister Eckhart, *Deutsche Predigten und Tractate*, quoted in Matthew Fox, "Meister Eckhart's Spiritual Journey," in Matthew Fox, ed., *Western Spirituality: Historical Roots, Ecumenical Routes*. Bear & Company, Inc., 1979. p. 240.

47. Fox, *Ibid.*, p. 240.

48. Catherine of Siena, quoted in Carola Parks, "The Letters of Catherine of Siena," in *Western Spirituality*, p. 255.

49. Gustavo Gutierrez, *A Theology of Liberation: History, Politics and Salvation*. Orbis Books, 1973, p. 204.

50. Thomas Merton, *Contemplation in a World of Action*. Doubleday and Company, 1971, p. 149.

51. Thomas Merton, "Contemplative Prayer," quoted in Kenneth Leech, *Soul Friend: The Practice of Christian Spirituality*. Harper & Row, 1977, p. 189.

52. Jacqueline McMakin and Rhoda Nary, *The Word for Stewards*. Christian Board of Publication, 1987, p. 33.

53. Dorothy Day, *The Long Loneliness: The Autobiography of Dorothy Day*. Harper and Row, 1952, p. 263.

54. Wes Michaelson, "Interview with Dorothy Day," *Sojourners*, December 1976, p. 18.

55. Cosby, *Ibid.*, p. 12.

56. Sallie McFague, *Models of God: Theology for an Ecological, Nuclear Age*. Fortress Press, 1987, p. xiii.

57. Thomas P. McDonnell, ed., *Through the Year with Thomas Merton*. Doubleday, 1985, p. 155.

58. A good resource for alternative lifestyle ideas is Alternatives, Inc., Forest Park, Georgia 30051.

59. Ronald J. Allen, speaking to the 1987 retreat of the Illinois-Wisconsin Ministers and Spouses of the Christian church (Disciples of Christ) at Eureka, Illinois.

60. Cosby, *Ibid.*, p. 13.

61. *A Spirituality for Our Times*. World Council of Churches, 1985, pp. 14–15.

62. Sallie McFague, *Metaphorical Theology: Models of God in Religious Language*. Fortress Press, 1982, p. 2.

63. Barbara Brown Zikmund, "The Trinity and Women's Experience," *The Christian Century*, April 15, 1987, pp. 354–356.

64. David Tracy and John B. Cobb, Jr., *Talking About God: Doing Theology in the Context of Modern Pluralism*. Seabury, 1983, p. 78.

65. *An Inclusive Language Lectionary, Reading for Year A*, Revised Edition, The Cooperative Publication Association, 1986, p. 5.

66.*Ibid.*, p. 10.

67. Phyllis Trible, *God and the Rhetoric of Sexuality*. Fortress, 1978, p. 200.

68. Eva Zabolai-Csekme, "A Woman Looks at Theology," *The Ecumenical Review*, Vol. XXVII, No. 4 (October 1975), p. 330ff.

69. Susan Brooks Thistlethwaite, "Inclusive Language and Linguistic Blindness," *Theology Today*, Vol. XLIII, No. 4 (January 1987), p. 536.

70. *Ibid.*, p. 537.

71. Rebecca Oxford-Carpenter, "Gender and the Trinity," *Theology Today*, Vol. XII, No. 1 (April 1984), pp. 16ff.

72. Letty M. Russell, *Feminist Interpretation of the Bible*. Westminster, 1985, p. 143.

73. Robert A. Bennett, "The Power of Language in Worship," *Theology Today*, Vol. XLVIII, No. 4 (January 1987), pp. 546ff.

74. Letty M. Russell, *Human Liberation in a Feminist Perspective — A Theology*. Westminster, 1974, p. 94.

75. Bennett, *Ibid.*, p. 547.

76. Oxford-Carpenter, *Ibid.*, pp. 7–25.

77. *An Inclusive Language Lectionary*, p. 10.

78. For a comprehensive treatment of a similar idea, see John H. Westerhoff, III, *A Pilgrim People: Learning Through the Church Year*. Seabury Press, 1984, pp. 85–97.

79. Dieter T. Hessel, *Ibid.*, pp. 269ff.

80. Ideas on combining a Shrove Tuesday Festival with intergenerational learning were given in a discussion with Richard Ziglar of Tulsa, Oklahoma.